KU-134-715

WORLD FAMOUS STRANGE TALES AND WEIRD MYSTERIES

WORLD FAMOUS
STRANGE TALES
AND WEIRD
MYSTERIES

Colin Wilson
with Damon and Rowan Wilson

Constable & Robinson Ltd
3 The Lanchesters
162 Fulham Palace Road
London W6 9ER

This edition published by Magpie Books,
an imprint of Constable & Robinson Ltd 2004

First published by Magpie Books 1992

Copyright © 1992 Constable & Robinson Ltd

All rights reserved. This book is sold subject to the condition
that it shall not, by way of trade or otherwise, be lent, re-sold,
hired out or otherwise circulated in any form of binding or cover
other than that in which it is published and without a similar
condition including this condition being imposed on
the subsequent purchaser.

A copy of the British Library Cataloguing in Publication Data
is available from the British Library.

ISBN 1-84529-162-X

Printed and bound in the EU

Contents

Chapter One

The Barbados Coffins

All students of unsolved mysteries encounter cases that defy their powers of explanation. For me, perhaps the most baffling is the mystery of the Barbados Vault.

The burial vault belonged to the Chase family, who were slave owners on the island of Barbados, in the Caribbean. In the early nineteenth century, the head of the family was a harsh and ruthless man called the Honourable Thomas Chase, who seems to have been a tyrant both to his slaves and his family. His daughter, Dorcas Chase, is believed to have starved herself to death because of her father's brutality. In July 1812, her coffin joined those of two others already buried in the vault – a woman named Goddard and a baby.

On 9 August 1812, the coffin of the Honourable Thomas Chase himself was carried down the steps to the family vault in the graveyard of Christ Church. It was encased in lead, and took eight men to lift. As the heavy stone slab was moved aside, and the lamplight revealed the interior, it was obvious that some intruder had already been inside. The baby's coffin was found upside down in a corner, while Dorcas Chase's coffin lay on its side. Only the coffin of Mrs Goddard was undisturbed.

The odd thing was that there was no sign of a forced entrance. But because Thomas Chase was a much-hated man, his surviving family members assumed that the desecration was the work of rebellious black slaves. Therefore the coffins were simply replaced, and the vault closed up again, and the marble slab sealed in place with cement. Only the negroes who carried Thomas Chase's coffin seemed alarmed; they seemed to suspect black magic.

Yet when the next burial took place, four years later in 1816, the vault was again in confusion, with all the coffins in different positions. And again, four weeks later, when a man murdered in a slave rebellion was buried there. Yet the cement round the marble slab was untouched. And the most careful examination of the vault revealed no other way of entering it.

When the next burial took place three years later, in July 1819, there was widespread curiosity, for the strange events had caused much gossip. Even when the cement was chipped away, the slab proved very hard to move. And this was because the heavy lead coffin of Thomas Chase was jammed against it. All the other coffins were in disorder, except that of Mrs Goddard, which had been left leaning against the wall.

The governor of the island, Lord Combermere, was present, and he ordered that the floor should be scattered with sand, which would show the footprints of any intruders.

Eight months later, in April 1820, the guests at a dinner party at Lord Combermere's began to discuss the vault, and it was decided to re-open it. Yet again, all the coffins – except Mrs Goddard's – were scattered. And the sand on the floor was undisturbed. This time, Lord Combermere ordered that the coffins should be buried elsewhere. The tomb has remained empty ever since.

This is a case where all the natural explanations fail. The coffins cannot have been disturbed by floods, or Mrs Goddard's wooden coffin would have been disturbed. There were no earth tremors at the time that could explain the mystery. But "supernatural" explanations are also inadequate. The only "mischievous" spirit known to psychical research is the poltergeist, which causes loud noises and sometimes throws objects around.

A few experts on the paranormal believe that poltergeists

are spirits of the dead; others believe that the phenomena are somehow caused by the unconscious mind of a psychologically disturbed adolescent, and are a mysterious form of "mind over matter". The one thing that is certain is that they do not take place in empty houses or burial vaults.

A more recent explanation was put forward by a sceptical investigator called Joe Nickell, in a book called *Secrets of the Supernatural*. Investigating a case of a mysterious silver mine in Kentucky, Nickell discovered that the whole story was invented by Freemasons, a "secret" Christian fraternity whose rituals are full of symbolism. In this case, the "silver mine" symbolized Freemasonry itself. Could this also be the explanation of the Barbados mystery? Nickell's researches revealed that Lord Combermere *was* a Freemason, and he believes that this is enough to prove his case that the whole story was pure invention. He ignores the various accounts of the events by the Reverend Thomas Orderson, the local vicar who witnessed the disturbances. Nickell's attempts to prove that Orderson was a Freemason ended in failure.

In any case, he totally fails to explain just *why* a vicar, a governor and many other respectable people should decide to invent a lie in order to "symbolize Freemasonry". It would have been a totally meaningless thing to do.

The frightened negroes who carried the coffins into the vault were convinced that the explanation lay in voodoo – or black magic – that "voodoo magicians" had deliberately sent spirits to throw the coffins around. Some psychical investigators believe that "black magic" *can* work, and I am personally willing to believe they may be correct. But even if "voodoo" *is* the explanation, the Barbados case is unique; at least, I have never heard of another like it.

Let us say simply that neither sceptics nor believers have ever succeeded in explaining the riddle of the Chase family vault.

During the 1930s the United Fruit Company cleared vast areas of Costa Rican jungle in order to create banana plantations. When the workers came to burn and hack the vegetation of the Diquis Delta they were surprised to discover vast numbers of granite spheres, entirely buried in the foliage. They ranged from the small, about the size of a cricket ball and weighing a few pounds, to the enormous, eight feet in diameter and weighing sixteen tons. Many were rounded with astonishing accuracy, appearing to the eye to be perfectly spherical, yet their surfaces showed no sign of mechanical grinding. They were clearly man-made, not least because the granite from which they were cut did not occur naturally where they were found. Locals broke some open, believing them to contain treasure.

They remain entirely mysterious. Some were found over graves, others arranged in lines, curves and triangles. Pottery found underneath them dates from many centuries, the latest being the sixteenth. That they had some religious significance seems to be the only certain conclusion, for it is difficult to imagine a practical use for such an array of objects.

The more impressive of the balls now adorn the gardens of wealthy locals.

Chapter Two

The Bermuda Triangle

On the afternoon of 5 December 1945 five Avenger torpedo-bombers took off from Fort Lauderdale, Florida, for a routine two-hour patrol over the Atlantic. Flight 19 was commanded by Flight Leader Charles Taylor; the other four pilots were trainees, flying what is known as a "milk run" that is, a flight whose purpose is simply to increase their number of hours in the air without instructors. By 2.15 the planes were well over the Atlantic, and following their usual patrol route. The weather was warm and clear.

At 3.45 the control tower received a message from Taylor: "This is an emergency. We seem to be off course. We cannot see land . . . repeat . . . we cannot see land."

"What is your position?"

"We're not sure of our position. We can't be sure where we are. We seem to be lost."

"Head due west," replied the tower.

"We don't know which way is west. Everything is wrong . . . strange. We can't be sure of any direction. Even the ocean doesn't look as it should."

The tower was perplexed; even if some kind of magnetic interference caused all five compasses to malfunction, the pilot should still be able to see the sun low in the western sky. Radio contact was now getting worse, restricting any messages to short sentences. At one point the tower picked up one pilot speaking to another, saying that all the instruments in his plane were "going crazy". At 4 o'clock the flight leader decided to hand over to someone else. At 4.25 the new leader told the tower: "We're not certain where we are."

Unless the planes could find their way back over land

during the next four hours, they would run out of fuel and be forced to land in the sea. At 6.27 a rescue mission was launched. A giant Martin Mariner flying-boat, with a crew of thirteen, took off towards the last reported position of the flight. Twenty-three minutes later, the sky to the east was lit briefly by a bright orange flash. Neither the Martin Mariner nor the five Avengers ever returned. They vanished completely, as other planes and ships have vanished in the area that has become known as "the Devil's Triangle" and "the Bermuda Triangle".

What finally happened to the missing aircraft is certainly no mystery. The weather became worse during the course of that afternoon; ships reported "high winds and tremendous seas". Flight 19 and its would-be rescuer must have run out of fuel and landed in the sea. The mystery is *why* they became so completely lost and confused. Even if the navigation instruments had ceased to function, and visibility had become restricted to a few yards, it should have been possible to fly up above the clouds to regain their bearings.

What seems stranger still is that this tragedy should have failed to alert the authorities that there was something frightening and dangerous about the stretch of ocean between Florida and the Bahamas – a chain of islands that begins a mere fifty miles off the coast of Florida. But then the authorities no doubt took the view of many more recent sceptics, that the disappearance was a rather complex accident, due to a number of chance factors: bad weather, electrical interference with the compasses, the inexperience of some of the pilots and the fact that the flight leader, Charles Taylor, had only recently been posted to Fort Lauderdale and was unfamiliar with the area.

Similar explanations were adopted to explain a number of similar tragedies during the next two decades: the disappearance of a Superfortress in 1947, of a four-engined Tudor IV in January 1948, of a DC3 in December 1948, of another Tudor IV in 1949, of a Globemaster in 1950, of a British York transport plane in 1952, of a Navy Super Constellation in 1954, of another Martin seaplane in 1956, of an Air Force tanker in 1962, of two Stratotankers in 1963, of a flying boxcar in 1965, of a civilian cargo plane in 1966, another cargo plane in 1967, and yet another in 1973 . . . The total number of lives lost in all these disappearances was well in excess of two hundred. Oddly enough, the first person to realize that all this amounted to a frightening mystery was a journalist called Vincent Gaddis; it was in February 1964 that his article "The Deadly Bermuda Triangle" appeared in the American *Argosy* magazine, and bestowed the now familiar name on that mysterious stretch of ocean. A year later, in a book about sea mysteries called *Invisible Horizons*, Gaddis included his article in a chapter called "The Triangle of Death". His chapter also contained a long list of ships which had vanished in the area, beginning with the *Rosalie*, which vanished in 1840, and ending with the yacht *Connemara IV* in 1956. In the final chapter Gaddis entered the realm of science fiction, and speculated on "space-time continua [that] may exist around us on the earth, interpenetrating our known world", implying that perhaps some of the missing planes and ships had vanished down a kind of fourth-dimensional plughole.

Soon after the publication of his book Gaddis received a letter from a man called Gerald Hawkes, who told of his own experience in the Bermuda Triangle in April 1952. On a flight from Idlewild Airport (now Kennedy) to Bermuda, Hawkes's plane suddenly dropped about two hundred feet. This was not a nose-dive, but felt as if he had suddenly fallen down a lift-shaft in the air; then the plane shot back up again. "It was as if a giant hand was holding the plane and jerking it up and down," and the wings seemed to flap like the wings of a bird. The captain then told them that he was unable to find Bermuda, and that the operator was unable to make radio contact with either the US or Bermuda. An hour or so later the plane made contact with a radio ship, and was able to get its bearings and fly to Bermuda. As they climbed out of the plane they observed that it was a clear and starry night, with no wind. The writer concluded that he was still wondering whether he was caught in an area "where time and space seem to disappear".

Now, all pilots know about air pockets, where a sudden change in pressure causes the plane to lurch and fall, and about air turbulence which causes the wings of a plane to "flap". What seems odd about this case is the total radio blackout.

This was an anomaly that had also struck students of UFOs or flying saucers, who had been creating extraordinary theories ever since that day in June 1947 when a pilot named Kenneth Arnold saw nine shining discs moving against the background of Mount Rainier in Washington State. The flying-saucer enthusiasts now produced the interesting notion that the surface of our earth has a number of strange "vortices", whirlpools where gravity and terrestrial magnetism are inexplicably weaker than usual. And if extra-terrestrial intelligences happened to know about these whirlpools, they might well find them ideal for collecting human specimens to be studied at leisure upon their distant planet . . .

Ivan Sanderson, a friend of Gaddis's and a student of earth mysteries, felt that this was going too far. His training had been scientific, so he began by taking a map of the world, and marking on it a number of areas where strange disappearances had occurred. There was, for example, another "Devil's Triangle" south of the Japanese island of Honshu where ships and planes had vanished. A correspondent told Sanderson about a strange experience on a flight to Guam, in the western Pacific, when his ancient propeller-driven plane covered 340 miles in one hour, although there was no wind – about 200 miles more than it should have covered; checks showed that many planes had vanished in this area.

Marking these areas on the map, Sanderson observed that

they were shaped like lozenges, and that these lozenges seemed to ring the globe in a neat symmetry, running in two rings, each between 30°C and 40°C north and south of the equator. There were ten of these "funny places", about 72°C apart. An earthquake specialist named George Rouse had argued that earthquakes originated in a certain layer below the earth's surface, and had speculated that there was a kind of trough running round the central core of the earth, which determined the direction of seismic activities. Rouse's map of these seismic disturbance areas corresponded closely with Sanderson's "lozenges". So Sanderson was inclined to believe that if "whirlpools" really caused the disappearance of ships and planes, then they were perfectly normal physical whirlpools, caused, so to speak, by the earth's tendency to "burp".

Sanderson's theory appeared in a book entitled *Invisible Residents* in 1970. Three years later a female journalist, Adi-Kent Thomas Jeffrey, tried to put together all the evidence about the Bermuda Triangle in a book of that name, printed by a small publishing company in Pennsylvania. It was undoubtedly her bad luck that her book failed to reach the general public. For one year later in 1974 Charles Berlitz, grandson of the man who founded the famous language schools, once again rehashed all the information about the Bermuda Triangle, persuaded a commercial publisher, Doubleday, to issue it, and promptly rocketed to the top of the American best-seller lists. It had been twenty years since the disappearance of Flight 19, and ten years since Vincent Gaddis invented the phrase "Bermuda Triangle". But Berlitz was the first man to turn the mystery into a worldwide sensation, and to become rich on the proceeds.

Berlitz's *Bermuda Triangle*, while highly readable, is low on scholarly precision – it does not even have an index. One reason for its popularity was that he launched himself intrepidly into bizarre regions of speculation about UFOs, space-time warps, alien intelligences, chariots of the gods (à la von Däniken) and other such matters. And among the weirdest of his speculations were those concerning the pioneer "Ufologist" Morris K. Jessup, who had died in mysterious circumstances after stumbling upon information about a certain mysterious "Philadelphia experiment". This experiment was supposed to have taken place in Philadelphia in 1943, when the Navy was testing some new device whose purpose was to surround a ship with a powerful magnetic field. According to Jessup's informant, a hazy green light began to surround the vessel, so that its outlines became blurred; then it vanished – to reappear in the harbour of Norfolk, Virginia, some three hundred miles away. Several members of the crew died, others went insane. According to Jessup, when he began to investigate this story, the Navy asked him whether he would be willing to work on a similar secret project; he declined. In 1959 he was found dead in his car, suffocated by exhaust gas; Berlitz speculates that he was "silenced" before he could publicize his discoveries about the experiment.

And what has all this to do with the Bermuda Triangle? Simply that the Philadelphia experiment was supposed to be an attempt to create a magnetic vortex; like those suggested by Sanderson, and that (according to Jessup) it had the effect of involving the ship in a space-time warp that transported it hundreds of miles.

Understandably, this kind of thing roused sceptics to a fury, and there were suddenly a large number of articles, books and television programmes all devoted to debunking the Bermuda Triangle. These all adopted the common sense approach that had characterized the Naval authorities in 1945: that is to say, they assumed that the disappearances were all due to natural causes, particularly to freak storms. In many cases it is difficult not to agree that this is indeed the most plausible explanation. But when we look at the long list of disappearances in the area, most of them never even yielding a body or a trace of wreckage, the explanation begins to sound thin.

Is there, then, an alternative which combines common sense with the boldness necessary to recognize that all the disappearances cannot be conveniently explained away? There is, and it rests on the evidence of some of those who have escaped the Bermuda Triangle. In November 1964 a charter pilot named Chuck Wakely was returning from Nassau to Miami, Florida, and had climbed up to 8,000 feet. He noticed a faint glow round the wings of his plane, which he put down to some optical illusion caused by cockpit lights. But the glow increased steadily, and all his electronic equipment began to go wrong. He was forced to operate the craft manually. The glow became so blinding that he was dazzled; then slowly it faded, and his instruments began to function normally again.

In 1966 Captain Don Henry was steering his tug from Puerto Rico to Fort Lauderdale on a clear afternoon. He heard shouting, and hurried to the bridge. There he saw that the compass was spinning clockwise. A strange darkness came down, and the horizon disappeared. "The water seemed to be coming from all directions." And although the electric generators were still running, all electric power faded away. An auxiliary generator refused to start. The boat seemed to be surrounded by a kind of fog. Fortunately the engines were still working, and suddenly the boat emerged from the fog. To Henry's amazement, the fog seemed to be concentrated into a single solid bank, and within this area the sea was turbulent; outside it was calm. Henry remarked that the compass behaved as it did on the St Lawrence river at Kingson, where some large deposit of iron – or a meteorite – affects the needle.

Our earth is, of course, a gigantic magnet (no one quite knows why), and the magnetic lines of force run around its surface in strange patterns. Birds and animals use these lines of force for "homing", and water-diviners seem able to respond to them with their "dowsing rods". But there are areas of the earth's surface where birds lose their way because the lines somehow cancel one another out, forming a magnetic anomaly or vortex. The *Marine Observer* for 1930 warns sailors about a magnetic disturbance in the neighbourhood of the Tambora volcano, near Sumbawa, which deflected a ship's compass by six points, leading it off course. In 1932 Captain Scutt of the *Australia* observed a magnetic disturbance near Freemantle that deflected the compass 12°C either side of the ship's course. Dozens of similar anomalies have been collected and documented by an American investigator, William Corliss, in books with titles like *Unknown Earth* and *Strange Planet*. It was Corliss, who pointed out to me the investigations of Dr John de Laurier of Ottawa, who in 1974 went to camp on the ice-floes of northern Canada in search of an enormous magnetic anomaly forty-three miles long, which he believes to originate about eighteen miles below the surface of the earth. De Laurier's theory is that such anomalies are due to the earth's tectonic plates rubbing together – an occurrence that also causes earthquakes.

The central point to emerge from all this is that our earth is not like an ordinary bar magnet, whose field is symmetrical and precise; it is full of magnetic "pitfalls" and anomalies. Scientists are not sure why the earth has a magnetic field, but one theory suggests that it is due to movements in its molten iron core. Such movements would in fact produce shifting patterns in the earth's field, and bursts of magnetic activity, which might be compared to the bursts of solar energy known as sunspots. If they *are* related to earth-tensions and therefore to earthquakes then we would expect them to occur in certain definite zones, just as earthquakes do. What effects would a sudden "earthquake" of magnetic activity produce? One would be to cause compasses to spin, for it would be rather as if a huge magnetic meteor was roaring up from the centre of the earth. On the sea it would produce an effect of violent turbulence, for it would affect the water in the same way the moon affects the tides, but in an irregular pattern, so that the water would appear to be coming "from all directions". Clouds and mist would be sucked into the vortex, forming a "bank" in its immediate area. And electronic gadgetry would probably be put out of action . . .

All this makes us aware why the "simplistic" explanations of the problem all those books explaining that the mystery of the Bermuda Triangle is a journalistic invention are not only superficial but dangerous. They discourage the investigation of what could be one of the most interesting scientific enigmas of our time. With satellites circling the earth at a height of 150 miles, it should be possible to observe bursts of magnetic activity with the same accuracy that earth tremors are recorded on seismographs. We should be able to observe their frequency and intensity precisely enough to plot them in advance. The result could not only be the solution of the mystery, but the prevention of future tragedies like that of Flight 19.

Atlantis, the fabled lost continent, is first mentioned in Plato's dialogues between *Timaeus and Critias* written around 350 BC. There it is described as an enormous island "beyond the Pillars of Hercules" (the Straits of Gibraltar). On this island, civilization flourished long before Athens was founded in 9600 BC. The inhabitants were great engineers and aggressive warriors, harassing early European and Asian civilization until the Athenians finally conquered them on their own territory. At that point great floods overwhelmed the island, and both the Athenian army and the Atlantean civilization disappeared beneath the ocean in a day and a night.

Plato describes their culture and territory in detail. The city was eleven miles in diameter, formed from concentric rings of land and water. The Atlanteans were fed by crops grown on a large plain 230 by 340 miles located behind the city. Plato describes their buildings and their habits, setting the pattern for all future Utopian literature; indeed that is all that his writings on Atlantis were considered to be for roughly two thousand years.

Then in 1882, Ignatius Donnelly, American senator and well-read theorist published a book suggesting that Plato's "fable" was based upon a real civilization. He pointed out that scientists were now relatively certain that continents do appear and disappear beneath the waves, and that earthquakes and volcanic activity are capable of terrible damage. Much of the minutiae of Donnelly's argument proves to be inaccurate on close examination, but the idea that there was an entirely lost civilization beneath the waves proved too romantic to be stifled.

Atlantis has been associated with Lyoness, the sunken area of land between Land's End in Cornwall and the Isles of Scilly. Regular patterns of stones and carvings found on the sea bed near Bimini in the Bahamas have been identified as Atlantean. More plausible in some ways is Professor Angelos Galanopoulos's theory that Santorini in the Mediterranean was the source of Plato's story. Santorini is a volcanic island whose last major explosion was in 1500 BC. The eruption ripped the island apart and sent a tidal wave out that devastated many surrounding islands. Only two problems exist with this explanation. Firstly Santorini is a great deal too small to be Plato's Atlantis. Galanopoulos explains this by positing an error in transcription that multiplied all the figures Plato gives by a factor of ten. Indeed if one does remove a nought from all of Plato's measurements a fair approximation of Santorini's size does appear. The second problem is more difficult to resolve: Santorini is on the wrong side of the Pillars of Hercules. Galanopoulos's arguments on this score are more difficult to credit, as they place the Pillars of Hercules at the southernmost promontories of Greece. The area of Atlantean subjugation according to Plato does not marry well with this revision; Santorini is only marginally more likely as a sight for Atlantis than Cornwall.

The story of Atlantis still fascinates, but without more positive evidence it must be regarded as more a cautionary tale than a historical treatise.

Chapter Three

The Disappearance of Agatha Christie

In 1926 Agatha Chnstie was involved in a mystery that sounds like the plot of one of her own novels. But unlike the fictional crimes unravelled by Hercule Poirot, this puzzle has never been satisfactorily solved.

At the age of thirty-six, Agatha Christie seemed an enviable figure. She was an attractive redhead, with a touch of grey, and lived with her husband, Colonel Archibald Christie, in a magnificent country house which she once described as "a sort of millionaire-style Savoy suite transferred to the country".

She was also the author of seven volumes of detective fiction, of which the latest, The *Murder of Roger Ackroyd,* had caused some controversy because of its "unfair" ending. Yet the authoress was hardly a celebrity; few of her books achieved sales of more than a few thousand.

Then on the freezing cold night of 3 December 1926 she left her home at Sunningdale, in Berkshire, and disappeared.

At eleven the next morning, a Superintendent in Surrey Police was handed a report on a "road accident" at Newlands Corner, just outside Guildford. Agatha Christie's Morris two-seater had been found halfway down a grassy bank with its bonnet buried in a clump of bushes. There was no sign of the driver, but she had clearly not intended to go far, because she had left her fur coat in the car.

By mid-afternoon the press had heard of the disappearance, and were besieging the Christie household. From the

start the police hinted that they suspected suicide. Her husband dismissed this theory, sensibly pointing out that most people commit suicide at home, and do not drive off in the middle of the night. But an extensive search of the area around Newlands Corner was organized and the Silent Pool, an allegedly bottomless lake in the vicinity, was investigated by deep-sea divers.

What nobody knew was that Agatha Christie's life was not as enviable as it looked. Her husband had recently fallen in love with a girl who was ten years his junior – Nancy Neele – and had only recently told her that he wanted a divorce. The death of her mother had been another psychological shock. She was sleeping badly, eating erratic meals, and moving furniture around the house in a haphazard manner. She was obviously distraught, possibly on the verge of a nervous breakdown.

The next two or three days produced no clues to her whereabouts. When it was reported that some female clothes had been found in a lonely hut near Newlands Corner, together with a bottle labelled "opium", there was a stampede of journalists. But it proved to be a false alarm, and the opium turned out to be a harmless stomach remedy. Some newspapers hinted that Archibald Christie stood to gain much from the death of his wife, but he had a perfect alibi: he was at a weekend party in Surrey. Other journalists began to wonder whether the disappearance was a publicity stunt. Ritchie Calder suspected that she had disappeared to spite her husband, and bring his affair with Nancy Neele out into the open. He even read through her novels to see whether she had ever used a similar scenario. When the *Daily News* offered a reward reports of sightings poured in. They all proved to be false alarms.

Another interesting touch of mystery was added when her brother-in-law, Campbell, revealed that he had received a letter from her whose postmark indicated that it had been posted in London at 9.45 on the day after her disappearance, when she was presumably wandering around in the woods of Surrey.

In the *Mail* the following Sunday there was an interview with her husband in which he admitted "that my wife had discussed the possibility of disappearing at will. Some time ago she told her sister, 'I could disappear if I wished and set about it carefully . . .'" It began to look as if the disappearance, after all, might not be a matter of suicide or amnesia.

On 14 December, eleven days after her disappearance, the head waiter in the Hydropathic Hotel in Harrogate, North Yorkshire, looked more closely at a female guest and recognized her from newspaper photographs as the missing novelist. He rang the Yorkshire police, who contacted her home. Colonel Christie took an afternoon train from London to Harrogate, and learned that his wife had been staying in the hotel for a week and a half. She had taken a good room on the first floor at seven guineas a week, and had apparently seemed "normal and happy", and "sang, danced, played billiards, read the newspaper reports of the disappearance, chatted with her fellow guests, and went for walks".

Agatha made her way to the dinner table, picked up an evening paper which contained the story of the search for herself, together with a photograph, and was reading it when her husband made his way over to her. "She only seemed to regard him as an acquaintance whose identity she could not quite fix," said the hotel's manager. And Archibald Christie told the press: "She has suffered from the most complete loss of memory and I do not think she knows who she is." A doctor later confirmed that she was suffering from loss of memory. But Lord Ritchie-Calder later remembered how little she seemed to correspond with the usual condition of amnesia. When she vanished, she had been wearing a green knitted skirt, a grey cardigan and a velour hat, and carried a few pounds in her purse. When she was found she was stylishly dressed, and had three hundred pounds on her. She had told other guests in the hotel that she was a visitor from South Africa.

There were unpleasant repercussions. A public outcry, orchestrated by the press, wanted to know who was to pay the £3,000 which the search was estimated to have cost, and Surrey ratepayers blamed the next big increase on her. Her next novel, *The Big Four*, received unfriendly reviews, but nevertheless sold nine thousand copies – more than twice as many as *The Murder of Roger Ackroyd*. And from then on (as Elizabeth Walter has described in an essay called "The Case of the Escalating Sales") her books sold in increasing quantities. By 1950, all her books were enjoying a regular sale of more than fifty thousand copies, and the final Miss Marple story, *Sleeping Murder*, had a first printing of sixty thousand.

Agatha Christie divorced her husband (who wed Miss Neele) and in 1930 married Professor Sir Max Mallowan. But for the rest of her life she refused to discuss her disappearance, and would only grant interviews on condition that it was not mentioned. Her biographer, Janet Morgan, accepts that it was a case of nervous breakdown, followed by amnesia. Yet this is difficult to accept. Where did she obtain the clothes and the money to go to Harrogate? Why did she register under the surname of her husband's mistress? And is it possible to believe that her amnesia was so complete that, while behaving perfectly normally, she was able to read accounts of her own disappearance, look at photographs of herself, and still not even suspect her identity?

Lord Ritchie-Calder, who got to know her very well in later life, remains convinced that "her disappearance was calculated in the classic style of her detective stories". A television play produced after her death even speculated that the disappearance was part of a plot to murder Nancy Neele. The only thing that is certain about "the case of the disappearing authoress" is that it turned Agatha Christie into a best-seller, and eventually into a millionairess.

Chapter Four

The Devil's Footprints

The winter of 1855 was an exceptionally severe one, even in the southwest of England, where winters are usually mild. On the morning of 8 February Albert Brailsford, the principal of the village school in Topsham, Devon, walked out of his front door to find that it had snowed in the night. And he was intrigued to notice a line of footprints – or rather hoofprints – that ran down the village street. At first glance they looked like the ordinary hoofprints of a shod horse; but a closer look showed that this was impossible, for the prints ran in a continuous line, one in front of the other. If it was a horse, then it must have had only one leg, and hopped along the street. And if the unknown creature had two legs, then it must have placed one carefully in front of the other, as if walking along a tightrope. What was odder still was that the prints – each about four inches long – were only about eight inches apart. And each print was very clear, as if it had been branded into the frozen snow with a hot iron.

The villagers of Topsham were soon following the track southward through the snow. And they halted in astonishment when the hoofprints came to a halt at a brick wall. They were more baffled than ever when someone discovered that they continued on the other side of the wall, and that the snow on top of the wall was undisturbed. The tracks approached a haystack, and continued on the other side of it, although the hay showed no sign that a heavy creature had clambered over it. The prints passed under gooseberry bushes, and were even seen on rooftops. It began to look as if some insane practical joker had decided to set the village an insoluble puzzle.

But it was soon clear that this explanation was also out of

the question. Excited investigators tracked the prints for mile after mile over the Devon countryside. They seemed to wander erratically through a number of small towns and villages – Lympstone, Exmouth, Teignmouth, Dawlish, as far as Totnes, about halfway to Plymouth. If it was a practical joker, he would have had to cover forty miles, much of it through deep snow. Moreover, such a joker would surely have hurried forward to cover the greatest distance possible;

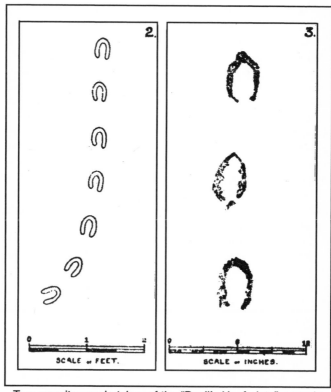

Two eyewitness sketches of the "Devil's Hoofprints", seen in Devon, 9 February 1855. *Fortean Picture Library.*

in fact, the steps often approached front doors, then changed their mind and went away again. At some point the creature had crossed the estuary of the river Exe – it looked as if the crossing was between Lympstone and Powderham. Yet there were also footprints in Exmouth, farther south, as if it had turned back on its tracks. There was no logic in its meandering course.

In places it looked as if the "horseshoe" had a split in it, suggesting a cloven hoof. It was the middle of the Victorian era, and few country people doubted the existence of the Devil. Men armed with guns and pitchforks followed the trail; when night came people locked their doors and kept loaded shotguns at hand.

It was another week before the story reached the news-papers; on 16 February 1855 the London *Times* told the story, adding that most gardens in Lympstone showed some trace of the strange visitor. The following day the *Plymouth Gazette* carried a report, and mentioned the theory of a clergyman that the creature could have been a kangaroo – apparently unaware that a kangaroo has claws. A report in the Exeter *Flying Post* made the slightly more plausible suggestion that it was a bird. But a correspondent in the *Illustrated London News* dismissed this idea, pointing out that no bird leaves a horseshoe-shaped print. He added that he had passed a five-month winter in the backwoods of Canada, and had never seen a more clearly defined track.

In the *Illustrated London News* for 3 March the great naturalist and anatomist Richard Owen announced dogmatically that the footmarks were those of the hind foot of a badger, and suggested that many badgers had come out of hibernation that night to seek food. He did not explain why all these badgers hopped along on one hind foot. (Five years later, he was to be equally dogmatic – and equally wrong – on the subject of Charles Darwin and the origin of species.) Another corres-pondent, a doctor, described how he and another doctor "bestowed considerable time in endeavouring to discover the peculiarities of this most singular impression" (the Victorians loved this kind of pompous language). He claimed that "on more minute examination of the tracks, we could distinctly see the impressions of the toes and pad of the foot of an animal". His own candidate was an otter. Another correspondent, who signed himself "Ornither", was quite certain that they were the prints of a Great Bustard, whose outer toes, he claimed, were rounded. Another gentleman, from Sudbury, said he had recently seen impressions of rats surrounding a potato patch, and that they looked exactly like the drawings of "the devil's footprints". He thought that the rats had been leaping through the snow, landing with their full body weight and producing a roughly horseshoe-shaped impression. A Scottish correspondent thought that the culprit could be a hare or polecat bounding through the snow. These suggestions are less absurd than they sound. They would certainly explain the most baffling feature of the footprints that they followed one upon another, as if made by a one-legged animal. But they still fail to explain why they continued for forty miles or so.

Perhaps the likeliest hypothesis is one put forward by Geoffrey Household, who edited a small book containing all the major correspondence on the matter.[1] He comments as follows, in a letter to the author:

> I think that Devonport dockyard released, by accident, some sort of experimental balloon. It broke free from its moorings, and trailed two shackles on the end of ropes. The impression left in the snow by these shackles went up the sides of houses, over haystacks, etc. . . . A Major Carter, a local man, tells me that his grandfather worked at Devonport at the time, and that the whole thing was hushed up because the balloon destroyed a number of conservatories, greenhouses, windows, etc. He says that the balloon finally came down at Honiton.

1. *The Devil's Footprints*, edited by G. A. Household, Devon Books, 1985.

This information is fascinating, and could well represent the solution of the mystery. But if so there is still one major anomaly to be explained. A glance at a map of the "footprints" will show that they meandered in a kind of circle between Topsham and Exmouth. Would an escaped balloon drift around so erratically? Surely its route would tend to be a more or less straight line, in the direction of the prevailing wind which, moreover, was blowing from the east.

The fact that it took a week for the first report of the mystery to appear in print means that certain vital clues have been lost for ever. It would be interesting to know, for example, whether the snow that fell that night was the first snow of February 1855. It had been a hard winter that year, and many small animals, including rats, rabbits and badgers, must have been half starved by February, and have been out looking for food. The letter to the *Plymouth Gazette* (dated 17 February) begins: "Thursday night, the 8th of February, was marked by a heavy fall of snow, followed by rain and boisterous wind from the east, and in the morning frost." Small animals had probably been out every night, but it was not until that Friday morning, with its fresh carpet of snow, that their tracks were noticed for the first time. Such tracks would have sunk deep into the soft snow, and would have been further deepened by the rain before they were frozen solid. This would explain why they seemed to be "branded" into the snow.

But if the ground was already covered with snow before the night of 8 February, then one more plausible theory would have to be abandoned. And in any case it fails to explain how the tracks managed to wander over rooftops and haystacks . . . At this distance in time, the only certainty seems to be that the mystery is now insoluble.

Strange Tales and Weird Mysteries

On 3 October 1984, a New Guinean giant fruitbat, an animal with a three-foot wing-span, was found clinging to the radiator of a car in Exeter, Devon. Its origins remain a mystery.

Chapter Five

Was Dillinger Shot?

Towards the end of his short life, John Herbert Dillinger was designated "public enemy number one", a distinction he shared with hold-up men like Baby Face Nelson, Pretty Boy Floyd and "Bonnie and Clyde". According to police records, Dillinger's sudden and violent end occurred outside the Biograph cinema in Chicago on 22 July 1934, when he was shot down by FBI agents. But since then there have been frequent doubts expressed about whether the man who died was actually the famous gangster.

John Herbert Dillinger was born on 22 June 1903, the product of an unhappy home life. When he was in sixth grade at school he was charged with stealing coal from the Pennsylvania Railroad's wagons to sell to residents of his Indianapolis neighbourhood. An angry magistrate shouted at him, "Your mind is crippled!"

When his father bought a small farm outside Mooresville, Indiana, Dillinger found country life intolerable. When a love affair went wrong he stole a car, drove to Indianapolis, and enlisted in the US Navy. During his four months as a sailor he was AWOL several times, and finally deserted in December. Back in Indiana, he married a sixteen-year-old girl and moved in with her parents. One day, after drinking in a pool hall, Dillinger and a former convict named Edgar Singleton concocted a robbery plan. They attacked a Mooresville grocer with a baseball bat, but the grocer fought back so vigorously that the would-be bandits fled. Dillinger was arrested on suspicion. When his father arrived at the gaol he admitted to the robbery, and the prosecutor promised his father that his son would receive a lenient sentence if he threw himself on the mercy of the court. It was Dillinger's bad luck to be brought before a severe judge, who fined him $200 and sentenced him to from ten to twenty years. Outraged at the broken promise, Dillinger made several unsuccessful attempts to escape from the State Reformatory at Pendleton. He also came under the influence of two determined bank robbers – Harry Pierpont and Homer Van Meter. Dillinger, who had homosexual tendencies, also had a lover in prison.

Released in May 1933, after a petition from the residents of Mooresville, Dillinger set out to organize a mass escape for his former friends, who were then in the state prison in Michigan City. He began committing a series of bank robberies, in one of them netting $10,600. But a girl cashier in a bank at Daleville, Indiana, told the police that she felt that Dillinger – who wore a straw boater to commit the robbery – was anxious not to frighten her. His sense of impudent humour revealed itself when, in the World Fair in Chicago in the summer of 1933, he asked a policeman if he would snap a picture of himself and of his girlfriend Mary Longnaker.

In September 1933 Dillinger tossed three guns wrapped in newspapers into the athletic field at Michigan City prison, but other inmates found them and handed them over to the Warden. Next, Dillinger bribed the foreman of a thread-making company to conceal loaded guns in a barrel that was being sent to the shirt shop in the prison. But by the time his friends broke out of gaol, Dillinger was already back in custody again – police keeping a watch on his girlfriend Mary had succeeded in arresting him. Ten men escaped. Shortly after, they rescued Dillinger from the Lima gaol, killing Sheriff Jess Sarber in the process. Eight days later, Dillinger and Pierpont walked into the gaol at Peru, Indiana, explained that they were tourists, and asked the police chief what precautions they had taken against the Dillinger gang. The police showed them their arsenal; Dillinger and Pierpont produced their guns, and left town with a car full of machine guns, shotguns and bullet-proof vests.

Now the "Dillinger mob" (as the press had already dubbed them) committed a whole series of robberies – the exact number is not certain – which made them notorious. When Dillinger was in a bank in Greencastle, Indiana, he saw a farmer standing at the counter with a pile of money in front of him. He asked, "Is that your money or the bank's?" "Mine," the farmer said. "Keep it," said Dillinger, and walked out with his sack full of the bank's cash. This kind of story brought Dillinger a reputation as a modern Robin Hood. The robbery brought the gang over $75,000. That winter they decided to move down to a warmer climate, and drove to Daytona Beach, Florida. But when they moved to Tucson, Arizona, their luck ran out: a fire broke out in their hotel, and a fireman discovered that their cases contained guns and ammunition. They were arrested and sent back to Indiana. Pierpont was charged with killing Sheriff Sarber.

On 3 March 1934 Dillinger made his spectacular escape from Crown Point gaol, Indiana, with a wooden gun that he had carved with a razor. The escape made him famous. (In fact, later investigation showed that Dillinger had somehow managed to get a real gun from somewhere.) Two weeks after the escape, Dillinger's fellow escapee, Herbert Young-blood, was killed in a battle with police. Dillinger quickly organized another gang, including Homer Van Meter and the short-tempered Baby Face Nelson (real name Lester Gillis). He also sent money for Pierpont's defence, but it did no good – Pierpont and another accomplice died in the electric chair. Soon after this Dillinger himself narrowly escaped death in a gun battle with police in St Paul, Minnesota. A month later police closed in around Dillinger's hideout at Little Bohemia Lodge, near Rhinelander, Wisconsin, but again the gang escaped. Only some innocent bystanders were shot. (The comedian Will Rogers joked that the only way Dillinger would get shot was if he got among some innocent bystanders some time.)

Under a plastic surgery operation to alter his face, Dillinger almost died, but the surgeon managed to pull his tongue out of his throat and got him breathing again.

With his new face, Dillinger had the confidence to go out into the open again. In Chicago he began to date a waitress named Polly Hamilton. Polly's room-mate was a forty-two-year-old woman called Anna Sage, who had served time for running a brothel. Anna was under threat of deportation, and when she learned Dillinger's identity it struck her that she might persuade the authorities to lift the deportation order if she betrayed him. Dillinger was now using the name James Lawrence.

So it came about that on the evening of 22 July 1934 Dillinger took his girlfriend Polly and Anna Sage to the Biograph cinema to see *Manhattan Melodrama,* starring Clark Gable. Anna Sage was wearing a bright red dress, in order to be easily identifiable. As they came out of the cinema FBI agent Melvin Purvis approached him and challenged him. The gangster pulled a Colt automatic from his pocket and sprinted for the nearest alleyway. Three agents fired, and Dillinger fell dead, with a bullet through his left eye; the man who had fired it was police detective Martin Zarkovich, of East Chicago. Later that day newsmen were taken to the morgue to see Dillinger's body. Foreign correspondent Negley Farson tells how the policeman pulled back the sheet over the naked body, and said grinning: "Well hung, isn't he?"

But was it Dillinger? The autopsy notes – made by Dr J. J. Kearns, the Cook County chief pathologist – reveal that the corpse's eyes were brown. Dillinger's were blue. The dead man possessed a rheumatic heart condition, chronic since childhood. Dillinger did not – he would not have been allowed to join the navy if he had. Lawrence was shorter and heavier than Dillinger, and had none of the scars and

wounds or birthmarks that Dillinger was known to have.

Crime writer Jay Robert Nash has argued that the FBI was duped into believing that the dead man was Dillinger, and that J. Edgar Hoover was too embarrassed to admit the mistake afterwards. "Jimmy Lawrence", according to Nash, was a small-time hoodlum, who came from Wisconsin to Chicago about 1930 and was often seen in the neighbourhood of the Biograph cinema. If Nash is correct, then we may assume that the "lady in red" deliberately "set up" the small-time hoodlum in a plot to provide Dillinger with a permanent escape. A photograph taken from the handbag of Dillinger's girlfriend Billie Frechette some time before his "killing" shows her with a man who bears an amazing resemblance to the corpse of James Lawrence. It seems possible, therefore, that she was also involved in the plot to take the heat off her former lover.

Within months Dillinger's gang was wiped out. Homer Van Meter was killed in an alley and Baby Face Nelson died in a gun battle, after killing two FBI agents. Harry Pierpont attempted to escape from the death house in the Ohio State Prison by carving a gun out of soap, but the ruse failed. He was electrocuted in October 1934.

What happened to Dillinger? A fellow gangster, Blackie Audett, who claims to have been in the Biograph cinema that evening, asserts in his book *Wrapsheet* that Dillinger married and fled to Oregon. He "disappeared" in the 1940s.

Chapter Six

The Mystery of
Eilean More

The Island of Disappearing Men

In the empty Atlantic, seventeen miles to the west of the
Hebrides, lie the Flannan Islands, known to seafarers as the
Seven Hunters. The largest and most northerly of these is
called Eilean More – which means in fact "big island". Like
the *Mary Celeste,* its name has become synonymous with an
apparently insoluble mystery of the sea.

These bleak islands received their name from a seventh-
century bishop, St Flannan, who built a small chapel on
Eilean More. Hebridean shepherds often ferried their sheep
over to the islands to graze on the rich turf; but they
themselves would never spend a night there, for the islands
are supposed to be haunted by spirits and by "little folk". In
the last decades of the nineteenth century, as Britain's sea
trade increased, many ships sailing north or south from
Clydebank were wrecked on the Flannans, and in 1895 the
Northern Lighthouse Board announced that a lighthouse
would be built on Eilean More. They expected construction
to take two years; but rough seas, and the problems of
hoisting stones and girders up a 200-foot cliff, made it
impossible to stick to the schedule; Eilean More lighthouse
was finally opened in December 1899. For the next year its
beam could be seen reflected on the rough seas between
Lewis and the Flannans. Then, eleven days before Christmas
1900, the light went out.

The weather was too stormy for the Northern Lighthouse

Board steamer to go and investigate, even though the light-house had been built with two landing-stages, one to the west and one to the east, so one of them would always be sheltered from the prevailing wind. Joseph Moore, waiting on the seafront at Loch Roag, had a sense of helplessness as he stared westward towards the Flannans. It was inconceivable that all three men on Eilean More – James Ducat, Donald McArthur and Thomas Marshall – could have fallen ill simultaneously, and virtually impossible that the lighthouse itself could have been destroyed by the storms.

On Boxing Day 1900, the dawn was clear and the sea less rough. The *Hesperus* left harbour soon after daylight; Moore was so anxious that he refused to eat breakfast, pacing the deck and staring out towards the islands; the mystery had tormented him, and now he was too excited to take food.

The swell was still heavy, and the *Hesperus* had to make three approaches before she was able to moor by the eastern jetty. No flags had answered their signals, and there was no sign of life.

Moore was the first to reach the entrance gate. It was closed. He cupped his hands and shouted, then hurried up the steep path. The main door was closed, and no one answered his shouts. Like the *Mary Celeste*, the lighthouse was empty. In the main room the clock had stopped, and the ashes in the fireplace were cold. In the sleeping quarters upstairs – Moore waited until he was joined by two seamen before he ventured upstairs, afraid of what he might find there – the beds were neatly made, and the place was tidy.

James Ducat, the chief keeper, had kept records on a slate. The last entry was for 15 December at 9 a.m., the day the light went out. But this had not been for lack of oil; the wicks were trimmed and the lights all ready to be lit. Everything was in order. So it was clear that the men had completed their basic duties for the day before tragedy struck them; when evening came there had been no one on the island to light the lamp. But the 15th of December had been a calm day . . .

The *Hesperus* returned to Lewis with the men's Christmas presents still on board. Two days later investigators landed on Eilean More, and tried to reconstruct what had happened. At first it looked as if the solution was quite straightforward. On the westward jetty there was evidence of gale damage; a number of ropes were entangled round a crane which was sixty-five feet above sea-level. A tool chest kept in a crevice forty-five feet above this was missing. It looked as if a hundred-foot wave had crashed in from the Atlantic and swept it away, as well as the three men. The fact that the oilskins belonging to Ducat and Marshall were missing seemed to support this theory; they only wore them to visit the jetties. So the investigators had a plausible theory. The two men had feared that the crane was damaged in the storm; they had struggled to the jetty in their oilskins, then been caught by a sudden huge wave . . . But in that case, what had happened to the third man, Donald McArthur, whose oilskins were still in the lighthouse? Had he perhaps rushed out to try to save them and been swept away himself?

All these theories came crashing when someone pointed out that the 15th had been a calm day; the storms had not started until the following day. Then perhaps Ducat had simply entered the wrong date by mistake? That theory also had to be abandoned when, back at Loch Roag, Captain Holman of the *Archer* told them he had passed close to the islands on the night of the 15th, and that the light was already out . . .

Then what if the three men had been on the jetty on a calm morning – which would explain why McArthur was not wearing his oilskins – and one of them had slipped into the water? Perhaps the other two had jumped in after him and been drowned. But then there were ropes and lifebelts on the jetty – why should men leap into the water when they only had to throw in a lifebelt?

Suppose the drowning man was unconscious, and could not grab a lifebelt? In that case only one of his companions

would have jumped in after him, leaving the other on the jetty with a rope . . .

Another theory was that one of the three men had gone insane and pushed the others to their deaths, then thrown himself into the sea. It is just possible; but there is not the slightest shred of evidence for it.

The broadcaster Valentine Dyall – the "Man in Black" – suggested the most plausible explanation in his book *Unsolved Mysteries*. In 1947 a Scottish journalist named Iain Campbell visited Eilean More on a calm day, and was standing near the west landing when the sea suddenly gave a heave, and rose seventy feet over the jetty. Then, after about a minute, it subsided back to normal. It could have been some freak of the tides, or possibly an underwater earthquake. Campbell was convinced that anyone on the jetty at that time would have been sucked into the sea. The lighthouse keeper told him that this curious "upheaval" occurs periodically, and that several men had almost been dragged into the sea.

But it is still hard to understand how *three* men could be involved in such an accident. Since McArthur was not wearing his oilskins, we can presume he was in the tower when it happened – *if* it happened. Even if his companions were swept away, would he be stupid enough to rush down to the jetty and fling himself into the sea?

Only one thing is clear: that on that calm December day at the turn of the century, some accident snatched three men off Eilean More, and left not even a shred of a clue to the mystery.

In the late eighteenth century a traveller's tale was passed around London. It told of two Welsh missionaries who, having been captured by American Indians and sentenced to death, began lamenting to each other in Welsh. The tribe of Indians were astounded: they too spoke Welsh. The missionaries were freed and received the Indians' heartfelt apologies.

The great Welsh Druid Edward Williams, or Iolo Morganwg, took the story so seriously that he raised backing for an expedition to investigate the Welsh Indians. The theory put forward for their existence traced their roots to the expedition of the Prince Madoc, who set sail westwards in the twelfth century and was never heard of again. Williams was eventually prevented from going on the expedition by failing health, but one of his followers, John Evans, did attempt the journey. He eventually died in New Orleans after many adventures, having been unable to locate the Welsh Indians.

Chapter Seven

Did Joan of Arc
Return from the Dead?

On 30 May 1431 Joan of Arc was burnt as a heretic by the English; she was only nineteen years old. She regarded herself as a messenger from Heaven, sent to save the French from their enemies the English (who were in league with the Burgundians who captured her). At the age of thirteen Joan began to hear voices, which she later identified as those of St Gabriel, St Michael, St Marguerite and St Catherine. When the news of the encirclement of Orleans reached her little village in Lorraine, Domremy, her voices told her to go to lift the siege. Her military career was brief but spectacular: in a year she won many remarkable victories, and saw Charles VII crowned at Rheims. Then she was captured by the Burgundians, sold to the English for ten thousand francs, tried as a witch, and burnt alive.

But that, oddly enough, was not quite the end of "the Maid". "Now one month after Paris had returned to her allegiance to King Charles", writes Anatole France, "there appeared in Lorraine a certain damsel. She was about twenty-five years old. Hitherto she had been called Claude; but now she made herself known to divers lords of the town of Metz as being Jeanne the Maid." This was in May 1436, five years after Joan had died at the stake.

It sounds very obviously as if some impostor had decided to pose as Joan the Maid. But there is some astonishing evidence that suggests that this is not so. Joan's two younger brothers, Petit-Jean and Pierre, were still serving in the army, and they had no doubt whatever that their sister had been burnt at Rouen. So when they heard that a woman claiming to be Joan was at Metz, and that she had expressed a wish to meet them, the brothers hastened to Metz – Petit-Jean was not far away, being the provost of Vaucouleurs. One chronicler describes how the brothers went to the village of La-Grange-aux-Ormes, two and a half miles south of Metz, where a tournament was being held. A knight in armour was galloping around an obstacle course and pulling stakes expertly out of the ground; this was the person who claimed to be their sister. The brothers rode out on to the field, prepared to challenge the impostor. But when Petit-Jean demanded, "Who are you?", the "impostor" raised her visor, and both brothers gaped in astonishment as they recognized their sister Joan.

In fact Joan was surrounded by various people who had known her during her spectacular year fighting the English, including Nicole Lowe, the king's chamberlain. If she was in fact an impostor, it seems absurd that she should go to a place where she would be sure to be recognized. (John of Metz was one of her first and most loyal supporters.) And the next day her brothers took her to Vaucouleurs, where she spent a week, apparently accepted by many people who had seen her there seven years earlier, when she had gone to see the local squire Robert de Baudricourt, to ask him to send her to see the Dauphin, the heir to the throne. After this she spent three weeks at a small town called Marville, then went on a pilgrimage to see the Black Virgin called Notre Dame de Liance, between Laon and Rheims. Then she went to stay with Elizabeth, Duchess of Luxembourg, at Arlon. Meanwhile her brother Petit-Jean went to see the king and announced that his sister Joan was still alive. We do not know the king's reaction, but he ordered his treasurer to give Petit-Jean a hundred francs. An entry in the treasury accounts of Orleans for 9 August 1436, states that the council authorized payment of a courier who had brought letters from "Jeanne la Pucelle" (Joan the Maid).

Did Joan of Arc Return from the Dead?

The records of these events are to be found in the basic standard work on Joan of Arc, Jules Quicherat's five-volume *Trial and Rehabilitation of Joan of Arc* (1841), which contains all the original documents. One of these documents states that on 24 June 1437 Joan's miraculous powers returned to her. By then she had become something of a protégé of Count Ulrich of Württemberg, who took her to Cologne. There she became involved in a clash between two churchmen who were rivals for the diocese; one had been appointed by the chapter, the other by the pope. Count Ulrich favoured one called Udalric, and Joan apparently also pronounced in his favour. But her intervention did no good; the Council of Basle considered Udalric a usurper, and the pope's nominee was appointed. The Inquisitor General of Cologne became curious about the count's guest (remember that this was at the height of the "witchcraft craze"), and was apparently shocked to learn that she practised magic, and that she danced with men and ate and drank more than she ought. (The magic sounds more like conjuring: she tore a tablecloth and restored it to its original state, and did the same with a glass which she broke against a wall.) He summoned her before him, but she refused to appear; when men were sent to fetch her the count hid her in his house, then smuggled her out of the town. The inquisitor excommunicated her. Back at Arlon, staying with the Duchess of Luxembourg, she met a nobleman named Robert des Armoires and – no doubt to the astonishment of her followers – married him. (The original Joan had sworn a vow of perpetual chastity under a "fairy tree" at Domremy.) Then they moved to Metz, where Robert had a house, and during the next three years she gave birth to two children.

Two years later, in the summer of 1439, the "Dame des Armoires" went to Orleans, whose magistrats gave her a banquet and presented her with 210 livres by way of thanking her for her services to the town during the siege. Oddly enough, these same burgesses had paid for Masses in memory of the Maid's death three months earlier; presumably they must have changed their minds in the meantime. After 1439 the Masses ceased.

After two weeks she left Orleans in rather a hurry, according to one chronicler, and went to Tours, where she sent a letter to the king via the Baillie of Touraine, Guillaume Bellier, who had been the Maid's host ten years earlier. Moreover, she soon afterwards went to Poitou, where she seems to have been given the nominal command of a place called Mans – presumably by the king she had enthroned. Then the king transferred this command to Joan's ex-comrade in arms, Gilles de Rais. Since the days when he had fought beside Joan before the walls of Paris, Gilles had begun to practise black magic – in an attempt to repair his fortunes, drained by his excesses – and had become a sadistic killer of children. In the following year, 1440, Gilles would be tried and condemned to be hanged and burned. Meanwhile – assuming he met the Dame des Armoires (which seems practically certain, since she had to hand over her command to him) – he seems to have accepted her as his former comrade-in-arms. He also placed her in authority over the men-at-arms.

In 1440 Joan finally went to Paris and met the king. And for the first time she received a setback; after the meeting the king declared her an impostor. It may be significant that he did so after the interview. Surely if he could see she was a fraud he would have said so at the time? He even attempted to practise on her the same trick he had tried at their first meeting eleven years earlier, concealing himself and asking one of his men to impersonate him. But as on the previous occasion Joan was not to be deceived; she walked straight up to the king and knelt at his feet, whereupon the king said: "Pucelle, my dear, you are welcome back in the name of God." It seems, to say the least of it, strange that he should then have decided she was an impostor.

And now, according to the journal "of a Bourgeois of Paris", Joan was arrested, tried and publicly exhibited as a malefactor. A sermon was preached against her, and she was forced to confess publicly that she was an impostor. Her story, according to the "Bourgeois of Paris", was that she had gone to Rome about 1433 to seek absolution for striking her mother. She had, she said, engaged as a soldier in war in the service of the Holy Father Eugenius, and worn man's apparel. This, presumably, gave her the idea of pretending to be the Maid . . .

But the whole of this story is doubtful in the extreme. To begin with, Joan then returned to Metz, and continued to be accepted as "la Pucelle". In 1443 her brother Pierre refers to her in a petition as "Jeanne la Pucelle, my sister", and her cousin Henry de Voulton mentions that Petit-Jean, Pierre and their sister la Pucelle used to visit the village of Sermaise and feast with relations, all of whom accepted her. Fourteen years later she makes an appearance in the town of Saumur, and is again accepted by the officials of the town as the Maid. And after that she vanishes from history, presumably living out the rest of her life quietly with her husband in Metz.

What then are we to make of the story that the king declared her an impostor, and that she admitted it publicly? First of all, its only source is the "journal of a Bourgeois of Paris". This in itself is odd, if she was involved in such a public scandal. Moreover, the "Bourgeois" was hostile to the earlier Joan, in the days before her execution. Anatole France mentions that the common people of Paris were in a fever of excitement at the news that the Maid was still alive and was returning to Paris. The University of Paris was still thoroughly hostile to the Maid, who had been condemned as a witch. Her sentence could only be reversed by the pope, and he showed no sign of doing this, in spite of a movement to rehabilitate Joan. So as far as the clerks and magistrates of Paris were concerned, the return of Joan would have been nothing but an embarrassment. As to those authorities of the Church who were trying to have the Maid declared innocent (they succeeded in 1456, and Joan was finally canonized in 1922), they would have found the return of their heroine –

alive, healthy and married – an obstacle to their patriotic campaign. The king must have found himself under intolerable pressure to declare Joan an impostor. After all, if *he* declared her genuine, then it was "official", and no one in France had a right to doubt her identity. Moreover, there would be some question of public recognition . . . On the other hand, if he expressed doubts about her, the whole scandal was defused. She could return home and drop out of sight. And everyone would be much happier. And that, it seemed, is precisely what happened.

Anatole France takes it for granted that the Dame des Armoires was an impostor. But then his biography of Joan of Arc is permeated with his famous irony, and takes the view that she was a deluded peasant girl; France was basically a disciple of Voltaire. The notion that she was an impostor is indeed the simplest explanation. But it leaves us facing the problem: why, in that case, did so many people who knew "the Maid" accept the Dame des Armoires as genuine? It is conceivable that her brothers may have decided that it would be to their advantage to have their famous sister alive, and so condoned the imposture. But why should so many old comrades have agreed to support the story?

The Dame des Armoires never as far as we know explained how she came to escape the flames. But then presumably she would not know the answer to this question. She would only know that she had been rescued, and that someone else had died in her place – perhaps another "witch". It is easy to see how this could have come about. We know that Joan was an extraordinarily persuasive young lady, and that dozens of people, from Robert de Baudricourt to the Dauphin, who began by assuming she was mad, ended by believing that she was being guided by divine voices. We know that even in court Joan declared that she could hear St Catherine telling her what to say. Even at her trial she had certain friends; a priest called Loyseleur was her adviser. When Joan complained about the conduct of her two guards the Earl of Warwick was furious, and had them replaced by two other guards – which suggests that the earl held her in high regard. So it would not be at all surprising if there was a successful plot to rescue her. And it is possible that the English themselves may have been involved in such a plot; when Joan was apparently burnt at the stake in Rouen the crowd was kept at a distance by eight hundred English soldiers, which would obviously prevent anyone coming close enough to recognize her. At the trial for her rehabilitation in 1456 the executioner's evidence was entirely second-hand, although three of Joan's comrades who were with her at the "end" – Ladvenu, Massieu and Isambard – were actually present. *If* Joan was rescued, presumably they also were involved in the plot.

The rehabilitation itself has its farcical aspects. It began in 1450, and Joan's mother was the person who set it in motion, supported by Joan's brother Pierre. We do not know whether Joan's mother accepted the Dame des Armoires as her daughter, but there can be no doubt that she lent credence to the claim by not denouncing her as an impostor. Yet now, she and Pierre joined in the claim that was based on the assertion that Joan was executed by the English in 1431. But then the aim of the rehabilitation was financial; Joan had been a rich woman, thanks to the generosity of the king, and the wealth remained frozen while Joan was excommunicated. So, whether or not Joan's family believed that the Dame des Armoires was the Maid, they now had good reason to try to have her rehabilitated even if it meant swearing that she was dead.

If the Dame des Armoires was genuine, she must have felt there was a certain irony in the situation. She had been an embarrassment to everyone during her first career as the saintly virgin warrior; now she was just as much an embarrassment as the heroine returned from the dead. It is thankless work being a saint.

Chapter Eight

The Loch Ness Monster

Loch Ness, the largest of British lakes, is twenty-two miles long and about a mile wide; at its greatest depth, it is 950 feet deep. It is part of the Great Glen, which runs like a deep crack right across Scotland, from one coast to the other; it opened up between 300 and 400 million years ago as a result of earthquakes, then was deepened by glaciers. At the southern end of the loch there is the small town of Fort Augustus; at the northern end, Inverness. Until the eighteenth century, the loch was practically inaccessible, except by winding trackways; it was not until 1731 that General Wade began work on the road that runs from Fort Augustus up the south side of the loch (although Fort Augustus was not so christened until 1742). But this steep road, which makes a long detour inland, was obviously not the shortest distance between Fort Augustus and Inverness; the most direct route would run along the northern shore. In the early 1930s a road was finally hacked and blasted out of this northern shore, and vast quantities of rock were dumped down the steep sides of Loch Ness.

The road had only just been completed in April 1933, and it was on the 14th of that month that Mr and Mrs John Mackay, proprietors of the Drumnadrochit Hotel, were returning home from a trip to Inverness. It was about three in the afternoon when Mrs Mackay pointed and said, "What's that, John?" The water in the middle of the loch was in a state of commotion; at first she thought it was two ducks fighting, then realized that the area of disturbance was too wide. As her husband pulled up they saw some large animal in the middle of the surging water; then as they watched, the creature swam towards Aldourie pier on the other side of the loch. For a moment they glimpsed two black humps, which rose and fell in an undulating manner; then the creature made a half-turn and sank from sight.

The Mackays made no attempt to publicize their story, but gossip about the sighting reached a young water bailiff, Alex Campbell, who also happened to be local correspondent for the *Inverness Courier*; he called on the Mackays, and his report went into the *Courier* on 2 May, more than two weeks after the sighting occurred. The editor is said to have remarked: "If it's as big as they say, it's not a creature it's a monster." And so the "Loch Ness Monster" acquired its name.

This was not, strictly speaking, the first account of the monster to appear in print. This distinction belongs to a *Life of St Columba* dating from about AD 565. This tells (in vol. 6, book 11, chap. 27) how the saint arrived at a ferry on the banks of the loch and found some men preparing to bury a comrade who had been bitten to death by a water monster while he was swimming. The saint ordered one of his own followers to swim across the loch. The monster heard the splashing and swam towards him, at which the saint made the sign of the cross and commanded the creature to go away; the terrified monster obeyed . . .

Other reportings down the centuries are more difficult to pin down; in his book on the monster, Nicholas Witchell mentions a number of references to the "beast" or "water kelpie" (fairy) of Loch Ness in old books between 1600 and 1800. And after Commander Rupert Gould published a book on the monster in 1934, a Dr D. Mackenzie of Balnain wrote to Gould claiming to have seen it in 1871 or 1872, looking rather like an upturned boat but moving at great speed, "wriggling and churning up the water". Alex Campbell, the water bailiff, reported that a crofter named Alexander MacDonald had seen the monster in 1802 and reported it to one of Campbell's ancestors. But hearsay reports like this inevitably led sceptics to suspect that local people, particularly hoteliers, had a financial interest in promoting the monster, so that by the mid-1930s "Nessie" (as she was soon christened in the area) had become something of a joke. In fact the first "modern" report of the monster had occurred in 1930; the *Northern Chronicle* reported that three young men who were out in a boat fishing on 22 July of that year, close to Dores, on the southern shore, saw a loud commotion in the water about 600 yards away, and some large creature swimming towards them just below the surface; it turned away when it was about 300 yards away. The young men commented that it was "certainly not a basking shark or a seal".

That summer of 1933 was one of the hottest on record, and by the end of the summer the Loch Ness monster was known to readers all over the British Isles; it was still to become a worldwide sensation.

By now the monster had also been sighted on land. On a peaceful summer afternoon, 22 July 1933, Mr and Mrs George Spicer were on their way back to London after a holiday in the Highlands. At about 4 o'clock they were driving along the southern road from Inverness to Fort William (the original General Wade road) and were on the mid-portion between Dores and Foyers. About two hundred yards ahead of them they saw a trunk-like object apparently stretching across the road. Then they saw that it was in motion, and that they were looking at a long neck. This was soon followed by a grey body, about five feet high (Mr Spicer said later "It was horrible – an abomination") which moved across the road in jerks. Because they were on a slope, they could not see whether it had legs or not, and by the time their car had reached the top of the slope it had vanished into the undergrowth opposite. It seemed to be carrying something on its back. They saw no tail, and the drawing that Commander Gould made later under their direction justifies Mr Spicer's description of a "huge snail with a]ong neck".

When Gould heard of this sighting he thought it was a hoax; but after he had interviewed the Spicers in London he had no doubt that they were telling the truth. The Spicers still seemed shaken and upset. It was later suggested the object over the monster's shoulder could have been a dead sheep. In 1971 Nicholas Witchell interviewed Mrs Margaret Cameron, who claimed to have seen the monster on land when she was a teenager, during World War I; she said, "It had a huge body and its movement as it came out of the trees was like a caterpillar." She also described it as being about twenty feet long, and said that it had two short, round feet at the front, and that it lurched from side to side as it entered the water. She and her friends felt so sick and upset that they were unable to eat their tea afterwards. Witchell also interviewed a man called Jock Forbes, who claimed to have seen the monster in 1919, when he was twelve; it was a stormy night, and he and his father were in a pony and trap when the pony shied, and they saw something large crossing the road ahead of them, then heard a splash as it plunged into the loch.

In November 1933 "Nessie" was photographed for the first time. Hugh Gray, an employee of the British Aluminium Company, was walking on a wooded bluff, fifty feet above the loch, near Foyers. He had seen the monster on a previous occasion, and was now carrying a camera. It was Sunday, 12 November 1933, a sunny morning, and Gray sat down for a moment to look out over the loch. As he did so he saw the monster rising up out of the water, about two hundred yards away. He raised his camera and snapped it while it was two or three feet above the surface of the water. It is not the clearest of all photographs – it is easy to focus attention on the dark shadow and to overlook the vague, greyish bulk of the creature rising from the water above it. This was only one of five shots; the others seem to have been even less satisfactory. Gray was so ambivalent about the sighting – afraid of being subjected to derision – that he left the film in his camera for two weeks, when his brother took it to be developed. It appeared in the Scottish *Daily Record* and the London *Daily Sketch* on 6 December 1933, together with a statement from the Kodak film company that the negative had not been retouched. But Professor Graham Kerr, a zoologist at Glasgow University, declared that he found it utterly unconvincing as a photograph of any living thing. It was the beginning of the "debunking" of the monster, in which major zoologists were to be prominent for many decades to come.

And the sightings continued. The day after Hugh Gray had snapped the monster, Dr J. Kirton and his wife were walking down the hill behind the Invermoriston Hotel when they saw the monster swimming away from them. They saw a rounded back with a protuberance in the middle, "like the rear view of a duck in a pond". Gould lists this as the twenty-sixth sighting of 1933. A week later, on the 20 November, the monster was seen lying motionless in the water for some ten minutes by a Miss N. Simpson, near Altsigh; she judged its length to be about thirty feet. Then she saw it swim underwater to the centre of the loch "at about the speed of an outboard motor boat".

On 12 December 1933 a firm of Scottish film producers, Irvine, Clayton and Hay, managed to film the monster in motion for a few seconds; unfortunately, the film shows little but a long dark shadow moving through the water.

The most famous photograph of the monster was taken in the following April – the celebrated "surgeon's photograph". On 1 April 1934 Robert Kenneth Wilson, Fellow of the Royal College of Surgeons, was driving northward with a friend; they had leased a wild-fowl shoot near Inverness, and meant to go to it and take some photographs of the birds. Wilson had borrowed a camera with a telephoto lens. It was early in the morning about seven and they stopped the car on a small promontory two miles north of Invermoriston. As they stood watching the surface they noticed the signs of "considerable commotion" that seem to herald the arrival of the monster, and the friend, Maurice Chambers, shouted, "My God, it's the monster." Wilson rushed to the car, came back with the camera, and managed to expose four plates in two minutes in such a hurry that he did not even look at what he was photographing. The serpentine head, not unlike an elephant's trunk, then withdrew gently into the water. Unsure as to whether he had captured anything, Wilson hurried to Inverness and took the plates to a chemist to be developed. They were ready later that day. Two proved to be blank; one showed the head about to vanish into the water. But the fourth was excellent, showing the dinosaur-like neck and tiny head.

Wilson sold the copyright of the photograph to the *Daily Mail* and it appeared on 21 April 1934, creating a sensation. It also aroused the usual roars of derision from the scientific establishment, who branded the photograph a fake, and

The Loch Ness Monster photographed on the 19th April 1934 by London Surgeon R. K. Wilson. *Fortean Picture Library.*

pointed out that the "surgeon" (who had withheld his identity) could be an invention of the perpetrator of the fraud. In fact, Wilson soon allowed himself to be identified, and his name appeared in Commander Gould's book *The Loch Ness Monster and Others,* which came out later the same year, with the "surgeon's photograph" as a frontispiece. (The fact that the photograph was taken on 1 April may have increased the general scepticism.) Many years later another monster-investigator, Tim Dinsdale, held the photograph at arm's length and noticed something that convinced him of its authenticity. When viewed from a distance, a faint concentric circle of rings is visible around the monster, while there is another circle in the background, as if some other part of the body is just below the surface. No one, Dinsdale pointed out, would take the trouble to fake a detail that is almost invisible to the eye. Another piece of evidence in favour of its authenticity emerged in 1972, when the photograph was subjected to the computer-enhancement process at NASA; the improved picture showed signs of whiskers hanging down from the lower jaw.

In July 1934 a team of fourteen men was hired by Sir Edward Mountain, at a wage of £2 per week per man, to spend five weeks standing on the shores of the loch, armed with cameras. Five promising photographs were taken; four of them only showed a dark wake, which could have been caused by a boat; the fifth showed a head disappearing in a splash of spray. After the watchers had been paid off, Captain James Frazer, who had been in charge of the expedition, succeeded in shooting several feet of film from a position just above Castle Urquhart. It showed an object like an upturned, flat-bottomed boat, about fifteen feet long; it disappeared in a spume of spray. Zoologists who viewed the film said that the creature was a seal. Captain Frazer later admitted that he had to endure a great deal of ridicule.

Sightings continued, and more photographs were taken; but the general public had ceased to be deeply interested in the monster. After the initial excitement, most people were willing to accept the view of sceptics that the monster had been a cynical invention of people involved in the Highland tourist business; if so, it had certainly succeeded, for Loch Ness hotels were crowded throughout the summer. One of the most interesting sightings of 1934 went virtually unnoticed. On 26 May Brother Richard Horan, of St Benedict's Abbey, was working in the abbey boathouse when he heard a noise in the water, and saw the monster looking at him from a distance of about thirty yards. It had a graceful neck with a broad white stripe down its front, and a muzzle like a seal's. Three other people corroborated his sighting. In the December of the following year, a Miss Rena Mackenzie also saw the monster fairly close, and noted that its head seemed tiny, and that the underside of its throat was white. A man named John Maclean, who saw the monster in July 1938, saw the head and neck only twenty yards away, and said that it was obviously in the act of swallowing food, opening and closing its mouth, and tossing back its head "in exactly the same manner that a cormorant does after it has swallowed a fish". When the creature dived Maclean and his wife saw two humps. They described it as being about eighteen feet long, and said that at close quarters its skin was dark brown and "like that of a horse when wet and glistening". Each of these sightings enables us to form a clearer picture of the monster. And in July 1958 the water bailiff Alex Campbell had a sighting which confirmed something he had believed for many years – that there must be more than one of the creatures; he saw one lying quietly near St Benedict's Abbey while another (visible as a large black hump) headed across the loch, churning the surface of the water. (Many accounts indicate that the animals can move at high speed.)

During World War II interest in the monster (or monsters) waned, although sightings continued to be reported. In 1943 Commander Russell Flint, in charge of a motor launch passing through Loch Ness on its way to Swansea, reported a tremendous jolt that convinced the crew that they had struck some floating debris. In fact, they saw the monster disappearing in a flurry of water. His signal to the Admiralty, reporting that he had sustained damage to the starboard bow after a collision with the Loch Ness monster, earned him in response "a bit of a blast".

In November 1950 the *Daily Herald* ran a story headed "The Secret of Loch Ness", alleging that dozens of eight-foot-diameter mines had been anchored on the floor of the loch since 1918, some at a depth of a mile. (The *Herald* stated that at its greatest depth, the loch is seven miles deep.) The story apparently had some slight basis in fact; mines *had* been laid in 1918 by HMS *Welbeck* – Hugh Gray, who later took the first monster photograph, was on board – but when a vessel went to collect them in 1922, only the anchors remained. The mines, which were designed to have a life of only a few years, were probably at the bottom. Certainly none of the photographs looks in the least like an eight-foot mine, even one with horns.

In the following year another monster photograph was taken by a woodsman named Lachlan Stuart. He was about to milk a cow early on 14 July 1951 when he saw something moving fast down the loch, so fast that he at first thought it was a speedboat. He grabbed his camera, rushed down the hill, and snapped the monster when it was only fifty yards offshore. The result was a photograph showing three distinct humps.

Four years later a bank manager named Peter Macnab was on his way back from a holiday in the north of Scotland, and pulled up his car just above Urquhart Castle. It was a calm, warm afternoon – 29 July 1955 – and he saw a movement in the still water near the castle; he hastily raised his camera, and took a photograph which has joined the "surgeon's photograph" and the Lachlan Stuart photograph as one of the classic views of the monster. But he was so anxious to avoid ridicule that he released the picture only three years later, in 1958.

Before that happened, interest in the case had been revived by the best book on it so far – *More Than a Legend*, published in 1957. The author was Constance Whyte, wife of the manager of the Caledonian canal, who became interested in the monster after she was asked to write an article about it for a small local magazine. Mrs Whyte interviewed every witness she could find, and produced the first overall survey of the evidence since Rupert Gould's book of 1934. *More Than a Legend* aroused widespread interest, the author was deluged with correspondence, and once again the Loch Ness monster was news. What Mrs Whyte had done, with her careful research, was to refute the idea that the monster was a joke, or the invention of the Scottish Tourist Board. No one who reads her book can end with the slightest doubt that the monster really exists, and that it shows itself with a fair degree of frequency.

The immediate result was a new generation of "monster-hunters". One of these, Frank Searle, was a manager for a firm of fruiterers in London; he bought Constance Whyte's book, and in 1958 decided to camp by Loch Ness. From then on he returned again and again. In June 1965 he was parked in a lay-by near Invermoriston and chatting to some hitch-hikers when he saw a dark object break the surface, and realized he had at last seen the monster. His excitement was so great that in 1969 he gave up his job and pitched his tent by Loch Ness, where he was to remain for the next four years. In August 1971 he saw the tail at close quarters as the monster dived; his impression was of an alligator's tail, "seven feet long, dark and nobbly on top, smooth dirty white underneath". In November 1971 he got his first photograph of the monster – a dark hump in a swirl of water; he admitted that it was "inconclusive". But in the following five years he obtained at least ten of the best pictures of the monster taken so far, including one showing the swan-like neck rising out of the water, and another showing both the neck and one of the humps; these were published in his *Nessie: Seven Years in Search of the Monster* in 1976. During that time his tent had become a "Mecca for visitors" – mostly directed to him by the Scottish Tourist Board – and in 1975 he estimated that he had seen twenty-five thousand in eight months. On 7 June 1974, together with a girl visitor from Quebec, he had a memorable sighting. As they approached a barbed-wire fence near Foyers, they noticed a splashing sound. They crept up and peered over the fence, "and saw two of the strangest little creatures I've ever seen. They were about two feet in length, dark grey in colour, something like the skin of a baby elephant, small heads with black protruding eyes, long necks and plump bodies. They had snake-like tails which were wrapped along their sides, and on each side of the body, two stump-like appendages." When he tried to get through the fence, the small creatures "scuttled away with a kind of crab-like motion" and were submerged in the loch within seconds.

But in his book *The Loch Ness Story* – perhaps the best comprehensive account of the hunt for the monster – Nicholas Witchell comments: "It is a regrettable fact which can easily be proved that these 1972 photographs have been tampered with. Mr Searle has also produced another series identical with the original shots in all respects except that an extra hump has been added to them by some process of superimposition or by rephotograph." And he adds: "Because of the highly suspicious content of some of Mr Searle's photographs and the inconsistencies of the facts surrounding the taking of them, it is not possible to accept them as being authentic photographs of animate objects in Loch Ness."

In 1959 an aeronautical engineer named Tim Dinsdale read an article about the monster in a magazine called *Everybody's*, and was intrigued. He spent most of that winter reading everything he could find; it was in the following February that (as already described) he looked at the surgeon's photograph, and noticed the circle of ripples that convinced him that it was genuine. In April that year Dinsdale went off to Loch Ness to hunt the monster. But after five days he had still seen nothing. On the day before he was due to return home he was approaching his hotel in Foyers when he saw something out in the loch; his binoculars showed a hump. He snatched his 16-mm ciné-camera and began to film as the creature swam away. Then, almost out of film, he drove down to the water's edge; by the time he got there the creature had vanished. But Dinsdale had fifty feet of film showing the monster in motion. When shown on television it aroused widespread interest and – as Witchell says – heralded a new phase in the saga of the monster.

That June, 1960, the first scientific expedition to Loch Ness embarked on a month-long investigation, with thirty student volunteers and a Marconi echo-sounder, as well as a large collection of cameras. A ten-foot hump was sighted in July, and the echo-sounder tracked some large object as it dived from the surface to a depth of sixty feet and back up again. The expedition also discovered large shoals of char at a depth of a hundred feet – an answer to sceptics who said that the loch did not contain enough fish to support a monster; the team's finding was that there was enough fish to support several.

But Dr Denys Tucker, of the British Museum of Natural History, who had organized this expedition, did not lead it as he had intended to; in June he was dismissed from his job – as he believed, because he had publicly expressed his belief in the existence of the monster.

Dinsdale became a close friend of Torquil MacLeod, who had seen the monster almost out of the water in February 1960. MacLeod had watched it for nine minutes, and admitted being "appalled by its size", which he estimated at between forty and sixty feet. It had a long neck, like an elephant's trunk, which kept moving from side to side and up and down, and "paddles" at the rear and front. In August

1960 MacLeod had another sighting from the shore, while a family in a motor yacht belonging to a company director, R. H. Lowrie, saw the monster at close quarters for about a quarter of an hour, taking a few photographs. At one point they thought the monster was heading straight for them and about to collide; but it veered away and disappeared.

It was also in August 1960 that Sir Peter Scott, founder of the Wildfowl Trust, and Richard Fitter of the Fauna Preservation Society, approached the Member of Parliament David James and asked for his help in trying to get government assistance for a "flat-out attempt to find what exactly is in Loch Ness". In April 1961 a panel decided that there was a prima facie case for investigating the loch. The result was the formation of the Bureau for Investigating the Loch Ness Phenomena, a registered charity. In October 1961 two powerful searchlights scanned the loch every night for two weeks, and on one occasion caught an eight-foot "finger like object" standing out of the water. In 1962 another team used sonar, and picked up several "large objects"; one of these sonar recordings preceded an appearance of the monster on the surface.

In 1966 Tim Dinsdale's film was subjected to analysis by Air Force Intelligence, which reported that the object filmed was certainly not a boat or a submarine, and by NASA's computer-enhancement experts, who discovered that two other parts of the body also broke the surface besides the main hump.

In 1972, a team of investigators led by Dr Robert H. Rines took some remarkable underwater photographs, one of which showed very clearly an object like a large flipper, perhaps eight feet long, while a 1975 photograph showed a long-necked creature and its front flipper; this was particularly impressive because the sonar evidence – waves of sound reflected back from the creature – made it clear that this was not some freak of the light or a piece of floating wreckage.

Yet in spite of this, monster-hunters in the 1970s and 1980s began to experience an increasing sense of frustration. When Commander Gould had written his book in 1934 the solution of the problem seemed close; then it receded. Constance Whyte's book revived interest in the mystery, and when the Loch Ness Phenomena Investigation Bureau began to co-operate with the team from the Academy of Applied Science, and to use all the latest scientific equipment, it began to look as if the mystery was about to be solved once and for all. Yet at the time of this writing – eleven years after that remarkable underwater picture of the monster – there has still been no major advance. Nicholas Witchell triumphantly concludes his book *The Loch Ness Story* (1975) with a chapter entitled "The Solution", in which he describes his excitement when Rines telephoned him from America to describe the colour photograph of the monster; it contains the sentence: "With the official ratification of the discovery of the animals in Loch Ness, the world will lose one of its most popular mysteries." And he declares that it would be ignoble now to gloat about the short-sightedness of the scientific establishment for its sceptical attitude towards Loch Ness.

It is now clear that Witchell was premature. Most people still regard the question of the monster's existence as an open one, and the majority of scientists still regard the whole thing as something of a joke. In 1976 Roy Mackal, a director of the Loch Ness Investigation Bureau and Professor of Biochemistry at the University of Chicago, published the most balanced and thoroughgoing scientific assessment so far, *The Monsters of Loch Ness*. He turns a highly critical eye on the evidence, yet nevertheless concludes that it is now proven that "a population of moderate-sized, piscivorous aquatic animals is inhabiting Loch Ness". If the scientific establishment was willing to change its mind, this book should have changed it; yet it seems to have made no real impacts.

When the "monster" is finally identified and classified it

will undoubtedly be something of an anticlimax, and Loch Ness will probably lose most of its tourist industry at a blow. Half the fascination of the monster lies in the notion that it is terrifying and dangerous. In fact all the evidence suggests that like that other legendary marauder the "killer" whale, it will turn out to be shy, amiable and quite harmless to man.

Chapter Nine

The Mystery of the *Mary Celeste*

On a calm afternoon of 5 December 1872 the English ship *Dei Gratia* sighted a two-masted brig pursuing an erratic course in the North Atlantic, midway between the Azores and the coast of Portugal. As they came closer they could see that she was sailing with only her jib and foretop mast staysail set; moreover, the jib was set to port, while the vessel was on a starboard tack – a sure sign to any sailor that the ship was out of control. Captain Morehouse of the *Dei Gratia* signalled the mysterious vessel, but received no answer. The sea was running high after recent squalls, and it took a full two hours before Morehouse could get close enough to read the name of the vessel. It was the *Mary Celeste*. Morehouse knew this American ship and its master, Captain Benjamin Spooner Briggs. Less than a month ago both vessels had been loading cargo on neighbouring piers on New York's East River. The *Mary Celeste* had set sail for Genoa with a cargo of crude alcohol on 5 November, ten days before the *Dei Gratia* had sailed for Gibraltar; yet now, a month later, she was drifting in mid-Atlantic with no sign of life.

Morehouse sent three men to investigate, led by his first mate Oliver Deveau, a man of great physical strength and courage. As they clambered aboard they saw that the ship's decks were deserted; a search below revealed that there was not a living soul on board. But the lifeboat was missing, indicating that Captain Briggs had decided to abandon ship.

There was a great deal of water below decks; two sails had been blown away, and the lower foretop sails were hanging by their corners. Yet the ship seemed seaworthy, and was certainly in no danger of sinking. Then why had the crew abandoned her? Further research revealed that the binnacle, the box containing the ship's compass, had been smashed, and the compass itself was broken. Two cargo hatches had been ripped off, and one of the casks of crude alcohol had been stoved in. Both forward and aft storage lockers contained a plentiful supply of food and water.

The seamen's chests were still in the crew's quarters, an indication of the haste in which the ship had been deserted. But a search of the captain's cabin revealed that the navigation instruments and navigation log were missing. The last entry in the general log was dated 25 November; it meant that the *Mary Celeste* had sailed without crew for at least nine days, and that she was now some 700 miles northeast of her last recorded position.

Apart from Captain Briggs and a crew of seven, the *Mary Celeste* had also sailed with Briggs's wife Sarah and his two-year-old daughter Sophia Matilda. Faced with the mystery of why they had abandoned ship for no obvious reason, Morehouse experienced a certain superstitious alarm when Deveau suggested that two of the *Dei Gratia*'s crew should sail the *Mary Celeste* to Gibraltar; it was the prospect of £5,000 salvage money that finally made him agree to Deveau's scheme.

Both ships arrived in Gibraltar harbour six days later. And instead of the welcome he expected, Deveau was greeted by an English bureaucrat who nailed an order of immediate arrest to the *Mary Celeste*'s mainmast. The date significantly was Friday the 13th.

From the beginning the *Mary Celeste* had been an unlucky ship. She was registered originally as the *Amazon*, and her first captain had died within forty-eight hours. On her maiden voyage she had hit a fishing weir off the coast of Maine, and damaged her hull. While this was being repaired a fire had broken out amidships. Later, while sailing through the Straits of Dover, she hit another brig, which sank. This had occurred under her third captain; her fourth accidentally ran the ship aground on Cape Brenton Island and wrecked her.

The *Amazon* was salvaged, and passed through the hands of three more owners before she was bought by J. H. Winchester, the founder of a successful shipping line which still operates in New York. Winchester discovered that the brig – which had now been renamed *Mary Celeste* – had dry rot in her timbers, and he had the bottom rebuilt with copper lining and the deck cabin lengthened. These repairs had ensured that the ship was in excellent condition before she had sailed for Genoa under the experienced Captain Briggs – this helped to explain why she had survived so long in the wintry Atlantic after the crew had taken to the lifeboat.

British officials at Gibraltar seemed to suspect either mutiny or some Yankee plot – the latter theory based on the fact that Captain Morehouse and Captain Briggs had been friends, and had apparently dined together the day before the *Mary Celeste* had sailed from New York. But at the inquiry that followed, the idea of mutiny seemed to have gained favour. To back this theory the Court of Inquiry was shown an axe-mark on one of the ship's rails, scoring on her hull that was described as a crude attempt to make the ship look as if she had hit rocks, and a stained sword that was found beneath the captain's bunk. All this, it was claimed, pointed to the crew getting drunk, killing the master and his family, and escaping in the ship's boat.

The Americans were insulted by what they felt was a slur on the honour of the US Merchant Navy, and indignantly denied this story. They pointed out that Briggs was not only known to be a fair man who was not likely to provoke his crew to mutiny, but also that he ran a dry ship; the only alcohol on the *Mary Celeste* was the cargo. And even a thirsty sailor would not be likely to drink more than a mouthful of crude alcohol – it would cause severe stomach pains and eventual blindness. Besides, if the crew had mutinied, why should they leave behind their sea-chests together with such items as family photographs, razors and sea-boots?

The British Admiralty remained unconvinced, but had to admit that if the alternative theory was correct, and Briggs and Morehouse had decided to make a false claim for salvage, Briggs would actually have lost by the deal – he was part-owner of the ship, and his share of any salvage would have come to a fraction of what he could have made by selling his share in the normal way.

In March 1873 the court was finally forced to admit that it was unable to decide why the *Mary Celeste* had been abandoned, the first time in its history that it had failed to come to a definite conclusion. The *Dei Gratia's* owners were awarded one-fifth of the value of the *Mary Celeste* and her cargo. The brig herself was returned to her owner, who lost no time in selling her the moment she got back to New York.

During the next eleven years the *Mary Celeste* had many owners, but brought little profit to any of them. Sailors were convinced she was unlucky. Her last owner, Captain Gilman G. Parker, ran her aground on a reef in the West Indies and made a claim for insurance. The insurers became suspicious, and Parker and his associates were brought to trial. At that time the penalty for deliberately scuttling a ship on the high seas was death by hanging; but the judge, mindful of the *Mary Celeste's* previous record of bad luck, allowed the men to be released on a technicality. Within eight months Captain Parker was dead, one of the associates had gone mad, and another had committed suicide. The *Mary Celeste* herself had been left to break up on the reef.

Over the next decade or so, as no new evidence came to light, interest in the story waned. During the trial, when fraud was still suspected, a careful watch had been kept on the major ports of England and America. But there was no sign of any of the missing crew.

In the year 1882 a twenty-three-year-old newly qualified

doctor named Arthur Doyle moved to Southsea, a suburb of Portsmouth, and screwed up his nameplate. And during the long weeks of waiting for patients he whiled away the time writing short stories. It was in the autumn of 1882 that he began a story: "In the month of December 1873, the British ship *Dei Gratia* steered into Gibraltar, having in tow a derelict brigantine *Marie Celeste*, which had been picked up in the latitude 38° 40′, longitude 70° 15′ west."

For such a short sentence, this contains a remarkable number of inaccuracies. The year was actually 1872; the *Dei Gratia* did not tow the *Mary Celeste*, the latter came under its own sail; the latitude and longitude are wrong; and the ship was called plain English Mary, not Marie. All the same, when "J. Habakuk Jephson's Statement" was published in the *Cornhill* magazine in 1884 it caused a sensation, launching Arthur Doyle's career as a writer – he was soon using the name A. Conan Doyle. Most people took it for the truth, and from then on it was widely accepted that the *Mary Celeste* had been taken over by a kind of Black Power leader with a hatred of Whites. Mr Solly Flood, the chief investigator in the *Mary Celeste* case, was so indignant that he sent a telegram to the Central News Agency denouncing J. Habakuk Jephson as a fraud and a liar. From then on the *Cornhill* was willing to publish most of Conan Doyle's stories at thirty guineas a time instead of the three guineas he had been paid so far.

Doyle's story was the signal for a new interest in the mystery, and over the next few years there were a number of hoax accounts of the last days of the *Mary Celeste*. They told all kinds of stories from straightforward mutinies to mass accidents – such as everyone falling into the sea when a platform made to watch a swimming race gave way, or the finding of another derelict carrying gold bullion, which tempted Captain Briggs to leave his own ship drifting while he escaped in the other one. One author argued that all the crew had been dragged through the ship's portholes at night by a ravenous giant squid, while Charles Fort, the eminent paranormal researcher, suggested the crew had been snatched away by the same strange force that causes rains of frogs and live fish. Fort added, "I have a collection of yarns, by highly individualized liars, or artists who scorned, in any particular, to imitate one another; who told, thirty, forty, or fifty years later, of having been members of this crew." Even today the *Mary Celeste* often sails unsuspectingly into TV serials and Sci-Fi movies to become involved in time warps or attacked by aliens in UFOs.

In fact, a careful study of the facts reveals that the solution of this particular mystery is obvious.

The man most responsible for the perpetuation of the myth about the *Mary Celeste* was Conan Doyle: it was he who insisted that the ship's boats were still intact. This small inaccuracy made an otherwise simple problem virtually insoluble.

In fact, once we know that the boat was missing, we at least know one thing for certain: that the crew abandoned ship, apparently in great haste – the wheel was not lashed, an indication that the ship was abandoned in a hurry. The question then presents itself: what could have caused everyone on board to abandon the ship in such a hurry?

Captain James Briggs, the brother of the *Mary Celeste*'s skipper, was convinced that the clue lay in the last entry in the log, for the morning of 25 November 1872: it stated that the wind had dropped after a night of heavy squalls. James Briggs believed the ship may have become becalmed in the Azores, and started to drift towards the dangerous rocks of Santa Maria Island. The gash-marks found along the side of the *Mary Celeste* – which the British investigators had claimed were deliberately made by the ship's mutinous crew – may have been made when she actually rubbed against a submerged rock, convincing the crew that she was about to sink.

Oliver Deveau proposed that during the storms some water had found its way from between decks into the hold, giving the impression that the ship was leaking.

The Mystery of the *Mary Celeste*

Another popular explanation is that a waterspout hit the *Mary Celeste*. The atmospheric pressure inside a waterspout is low; this could have caused the hatch-covers to blow open and forced bilge water into the pump well; this would have made it look as if the ship had taken on six to eight feet of water and was sinking fast.

There are basic objections to all these three answers. If the ship scraped dangerous rocks off Santa Maria Island, then the lifeboat would have been close enough to land on the Island. Since no survivors were found and no wreckage from the lifeboat, this seems unlikely.

Oliver Deveau's theory has a great deal more in its favour. There have often been panics at sea. When Captain Cook's *Endeavour* was in difficulties off the coast of eastern Australia, the ship's carpenter was sent to take a reading of the water in the hold. He made a mistake, and the resulting hysteria might have ended with the crew leaving the ship if Cook had not been able to control the panic. On another occasion a ship which was carrying a hold full of timber dumped the whole lot into the sea off Newfoundland, before anyone realized that it would be next to impossible to sink a ship full of wood. But it seems unlikely that a captain of Briggs's known efficiency would allow some simple mis-reading to cause a panic.

The objection to the waterspout theory is that, apart from the open hatches, the ship was completely undamaged. If a waterspout was big enough to cause such a panic, it would surely have caused far more havoc.

In any case, the real mystery is why, if the crew left the *Mary Celeste* in the lifeboat, they made no attempt to get back on board when they saw that the ship was in no danger of sinking.

Only one explanation covers all the facts. Briggs had never shipped crude alcohol before, and being a typical New England puritan, undoubtedly mistrusted it. The change in temperature between New York and the Azores would have caused casks of alcohol to sweat and leak. The night of storms, in which the barrels would have been shaken violently, would have caused vapour to form inside the casks, slowly building up pressure until the lids of two or three blew off. The explosion, though basically harmless, might have blown the hatches off the cargo hold on to the deck in the positions in which Deveau later found them. Convinced that the whole ship was about to explode, Briggs ordered everyone into the lifeboat. In his haste, he failed to take the one simple precaution that would have saved their lives – to secure the lifeboat to the *Mary Celeste* by a few hundred yards of cable. The sea was fairly calm when the boat was lowered, as we know from the last entry in the log, but the evidence of the torn sails indicates that the ship then encountered severe gales. We may conjecture that the rising wind blew the *Mary Celeste* into the distance; while the crew in the lifeboat rowed frantically in a futile effort to catch up. The remainder of the story is tragically obvious.

In Peru, between the Andes and the Pacific, lies the Nazca Plain. It is a vast, flat expanse of sunbaked stones; and from the ground extremely boring. Fly over it however, and what seemed like abstract markings from ground level resolve themselves into complex drawings of a bird, a lizard, a monkey, a spider and many other stylized images. They have been created by moving the dark stones that litter the surface of the desert and revealing the lighter earth beneath. This has been done on a grand scale, some of the "drawings" are over a hundred feet long.

These markings are believed to have been made by the Nazcan Indians, a pre-Inca race, between 100 BC and AD 600. It has been suggested that they correspond to some astronomical alignment, but study has shown that the small extent to which they do could very easily be coincidental. Erich von Däniken, the God-as-Astronaut theorist, believes the lines to be landing strips from alien spacecraft. In his book *Chariots of the Gods?* he shows two parallel lines with a widened area halfway along one of them. This, he puts forward, is a runway with a flying saucer parking area. The picture is in fact one of the Nazcan birds' legs. The wide area is its knee, a space hardly large enough to park a bicycle in.

Von Däniken does raise an interesting question however. Short of building hot-air balloons, the Nazcan Indians could never have been sure that they looked as they intended. One can only conclude that the pictures are designed to be seen by the gods. Whether these gods drove spaceships or not is a matter for conjecture.

Chapter Ten

Where is the Mona Lisa?

The answer to the above question may seem self-evident: in the Louvre. But the matter is not quite as straight-foward as it looks.

The Mona Lisa is better known on the continent of Europe as "La Gioconda", or the smiling woman – the word means the same as the old English "jocund". It was painted, as everyone knows, by the great Italian artist Leonardo, who was born in the little town of Vinci, near Florence, in 1452. Mona Lisa (Mona is short for Madonna) was a young married woman who was about twenty-four when Leonardo met her. She was the wife of a man twenty years her senior, the wealthy Francesco del Giocondo, and when Leonardo started to paint her around 1500 she had just lost a child. Leonardo's biographer, Vasari, says that her husband had to hire jesters and musicians to make her smile during the early sittings.

For some reason Leonardo became obsessed with her, and went on painting her for several years, always dissatisfied with his work. This has given rise to stories that he was in love with her, and even that she became his mistress; but this seems unlikely. Leonardo was homosexual, and took a poor view of sex, writing with Swiftian disgust: "The act of coitus and the members that serve it are so hideous that, if it were not for the beauty of faces . . . the human species would lose its humanity." Yet there was something about Madonna Lisa that made him strive to capture her expression for at least six years – possibly more. His biographer, Antonia Vallentin, says she fascinated him more than any other woman he met in his life. He gave the unfinished portrait to Mona Lisa's

Leonardo da Vinci's painting in the Louvre, Paris.
Is it of Mona Lisa?

husband when he left Florence in 1505, but still continued to work on it at intervals when he returned.

In his *Lives of the Painters,* Giorgio Vasari says that Leonardo worked at the Mona Lisa for four years and left it unfinished. "This work is now in the possession of Francis, king of France, at Fontainebleau . . ." And this, we assume, is the famous portrait now in the Louvre. Yet this raises a puzzling question. Leonardo gave the portrait to the man who had commissioned it, Mona Lisa's husband, in 1505, and a mere forty or fifty years later, when Vasari was writing, it is in the possession of Francis I of France. Surely the Giocondo family would not part with a masterpiece so easily? Besides, the Louvre picture is quite obviously finished . . .

There is another interesting clue. In 1584 a historian of art, Giovanni Paolo Lomazzo, published a book on painting, sculpture and architecture, in which he refers to "the Gioconda *and* the Mona Lisa", as if they were two separate paintings. The book is dedicated to Don Carlos Emanuele, the Grand Duke of Savoy, who was a great admirer of Leonardo – so it hardly seems likely that this was a slip of the pen . . .

Two Giocondas? Then where is the other one? And, more important, *who* is this second Gioconda?

The answer to the first question is, oddly enough, in the Louvre. The world-famous painting, which has been reproduced more often than any other painting in history, is almost certainly not the Mona Lisa that we have been talking about.

Then where *is* the painting of the woman who so obsessed Leonardo that he could not finish her portrait? There is evidence to show that this original Mona Lisa was brought from Italy in the mid-eighteenth century, and went into the stately home of a nobleman in Somerset. Just before World War I it was discovered by the art connoisseur Hugh Blaker in Bath, and he picked it up for a few guineas, and took it to his studio in Isleworth. Hence it became known as the Isleworth Mona Lisa. It was bigger than the Louvre painting, and – more important – was unfinished; the background has only been lightly touched in. Blaker was much impressed by it. The girl was younger and prettier than the Louvre Mona Lisa. And Blaker felt that this new Mona Lisa corresponded much more closely to Vasari's description than the Louvre painting. Vasari rhapsodized about its delicate realism:

> The eyes had that lustre and watery sheen which is always seen in real life, and around them were those touches of red and the lashes which cannot be represented without the greatest subtlety . . . The nose with its beautiful nostrils, rosy and tender, seemed to be alive. The opening of the mouth, united by the red of the lips to the flesh tones of the face, seemed not to be coloured, but to be living flesh.

Sir Kenneth Clark, quoting this passage in his book on Leonardo, asks: "Who would recognize the submarine goddess of the Louvre?" To which Blaker would have replied: "Ah, precisely." But the description *does* fit the Isleworth Mona Lisa.

There is another point that seems to establish beyond all doubt that Blaker's picture is Leonardo's Mona Lisa. The painter Raphael saw it in Leonardo's studio about 1504, and later made a sketch of it. This sketch shows two Grecian columns on either side – columns that can be found in the Isleworth Mona Lisa, but not in the Louvre painting.

Blaker believes that the Isleworth Mona Lisa is a far more beautiful work, and many art experts have agreed with him. It is true that the Louvre painting has many admirers; Walter Pater wrote a celebrated "purple passage" about it in *The Renaissance* beginning, "She is older than the rocks among which she sits; like the vampire, she has been dead many times . . .", and W. B. Yeats thought this so beautiful that he divided it into lines of free verse and printed it as a poem in his *Oxford Book of Modern Verse*. On the other hand, the connoisseur Bernard Berenson wrote about it: "What I really saw in the figure of Mona Lisa was the estranging image of woman beyond the reach of my sympathy or the ken of my interest . . . watchful, sly, secure, with a smile of anticipated satisfaction and a pervading air of hostile superiority . . ." He felt the beauty of the Louvre Mona Lisa had been sacrificed to technique. No one could say this of the far more fresh and lively Isleworth Mona Lisa.

But if the lady in the Louvre is not Leonardo's Lisa del Giocondo, then who is she? Here the most important clue is to be found in a document by Antonio Beatis, secretary to the Cardinal of Aragon. When Leonardo went to the court of Francis I in 1517 he was visited by the cardinal, and the secretary noted down the conversation. The cardinal was shown works by Leonardo, including St John, the Madonna with St Anne, and "the portrait of a certain Florentine lady, painted from life at the instance of the late Magnifico Giuliano de Medici . . ."

In her biography of Leonardo, Antonia Vallentin speculates that this work *was* the Mona Lisa, and asks: "Did Giuliano [de Medici] love Mona Lisa in her girlhood . . . did he think with longing of her now she was married to Messer del Giocondo, and had he commissioned Leonardo to paint her portrait?" But this delightful romantic bubble is shattered by a mere consideration of dates. Giuliano de Medici, brother of Lorenzo the Magnificent, master of Florence, was murdered in Florence cathedral in 1478. The plotters – mostly rival bankers – hoped to kill Lorenzo too, but Lorenzo was too quick for them. All this happened in the year before Mona Lisa was born.

Then who *was* the lady that Leonardo painted at the orders of Giuliano de Medici? Almost certainly the answer is Costanza d'Avalos, Giuliano's mistress, a lady of such pleasant disposition that she was known as "the smiling One" – la Gioconda . . .

And so it would seem that the painting in the Louvre has been labelled "the Mona Lisa" by a simple misunderstanding. Its subject is obviously a woman in her thirties not, like Mona Lisa del Giocondo, in her twenties. Leonardo took it with him to France, and it went into the collection of Francis I, and eventually into the Louvre. The unfinished Mona Lisa stayed in Italy, was brought to England, and was purchased by Hugh Blaker in 1914. In 1962 it was purchased for some vast but undisclosed sum – undoubtedly amounting to millions – by a Swiss syndicate headed by the art-collector Dr Henry F. Pulitzer, and Pulitzer has since written a short book, *Where is the Mona Lisa?*, setting out the claims of his own painting to be that of Madonna Lisa del Giocondo. Pulitzer's contention is simple. There are two Giocondas for Madonna Lisa had a perfect right to call herself by her husband's name, with a feminine ending. But there is only one Mona Lisa. And that is not in the Louvre but in London.

Chapter Eleven

Orffyreus and the
Perpetual Motion
Machine

The dream of perpetual motion is undoubtedly a delusion. The law of the conservation of energy states that energy cannot be created or destroyed; in other words, you cannot get more energy out of a machine than you put into it. So it is irritating to have to admit that there is one well-authenticated story of a perpetual motion machine that has defied all attempts at explanation. It was invented by a man who called himself Orffyreus, and it is described in the Leipzig *Acta Eruditorum* for 1717.

Its inventor's real name was Johann Ernst Elias Bessler, and he was born in Zittau, Saxony, in 1680. When he decided to choose himself a *nom de guerre* he wrote the alphabet in a circle, then selected the thirteenth letter after each of the letters of Bessler; the result was Orffyre, which he latinized to Orffyreus. Like Leonardo, he seems to have been a man of many talents, and studied theology, medicine and painting as well as mechanics. And in his early thirties he announced that he had discovered the secret of perpetual motion.

Now, perpetual motion *sounds* a practical possibility. Suppose, for example, that you construct an upright wheel, which spins on a well-greased axle. If you stick a very small weight on the top edge of the wheel (say a piece of putty) it will descend by its own weight to the bottom, and will then continue on, through its own momentum, until it comes *very nearly* to the top again. Suppose one could think of some ingenious means to add just that tiny extra push which would carry it over the top, some method of making little weights alter their position on the rim of the wheel, for example . . . But in practice it proves to be impossible without cheating – that is, giving the wheel a tiny extra push.

In 1712 Orffyreus appeared in the town of Gera, in the province of Reuss, and exhibited a "self-moving wheel". It was three feet in diameter and four inches thick. When given the slightest push it started up, then quickly worked itself up to a regular speed. Once in motion it was capable of raising a weight of several pounds. And this in itself is incredible. If an empty spacecraft was drifting through space, far from the influence of any star, it would continue moving in a straight line for ever, because there would be nothing to stop it. (This is Newton's first law of motion.) Similarly, if a wheel was given the slightest spin in empty space, it would go on spinning for ever. But it could not be made to do any "work" – to raise a weight, for example. As soon as its original energy was exhausted, it would stop. Yet according to Orffyreus his wheel could not only keep on spinning for ever, but could also raise weights. This was done by winding a rope round the axis, with a weight attached to it.

Oddly enough, the burghers of Gera do not seem to have been impressed by his demonstrations. It may be simply that they were not sufficiently mechanically minded to realize that he was offering them an invention that could transform the world. (If rediscovered today, his secret would enable us to dispense with coal, oil and atomic energy.) Or it may have been simply that Orffyreus was a singularly irritating person, self-assertive, boastful and dogmatic. At all events, he made far more enemies than friends, and soon had to move on. He left Gera without regret, and moved to Draschwitz, near Leipzig, where in 1713 he constructed a still larger wheel, this one five feet in diameter and six inches in width; it could turn at fifty revolutions a minute and raise a weight of 40lb.

Then he moved again to Merseburg, and constructed a wheel six feet in diameter and a foot thick. A number of local "learned men" examined his wheel, agreed that it was not moved by any outer force, and signed a certificate to that effect. But this minor triumph moved Orffyreus's enemies to fury. One published a pamphlet offering Orffyreus a thousand thalers if he could make a wheel revolve in a locked room for a month. Another offered to construct a wheel – admittedly a trick – that would do everything that Orffyreus's wheel could do. And J. G. Borlach of Leipzig published a pamphlet in which he demonstrated (what is undoubtedly true) that a perpetual motion machine is against the laws of nature.

In that same year, 1716, Orffyreus left Merseburg for the small independent state of Hesse-Cassel, in which he was to score his greatest triumph. Here at last his luck seemed to change. The reigning Landgrave (or Count), whose name was Karl, was sufficiently impressed by the homeless inventor to make him a town councillor and offer him rooms in the ducal castle at Weissenstein. And during the year 1717 he constructed at the castle his largest wheel so far, this one being twelve feet in diameter and fourteen inches thick. In spite of its size, it was fairly light-weight. It was described in a letter to Sir Isaac Newton by a Professor Gravesande of Leyden,

> . . . a hollow wheel, or kind of drum . . . covered over with canvas, to prevent the inside from being seen . . . I have examined the axles and am firmly persuaded that nothing from without the wheel in the least contributes to its motion. When I turned it but gently, it always stood still as soon as I took away my hand . . .

When set in motion, the wheel revolved twenty-five or twenty-six times a minute. An "Archimedean screw for raising water" could be attached to its axle by means of a rope; in that case the speed dropped to twenty revolutions a minute.

The wheel remained on exhibition in the castle for several months, and was examined by many learned men, who all concluded that there could be no deception. Then on 31 October 1717 Orffyreus was requested to transfer the wheel to another room in the castle, presumably a larger one, "where there were no contiguous walls". On 12 November the Landgrave and various officials came to look at the wheel, observed it in motion for a while, then watched as the doors and windows of the room were tightly sealed, in such a way that no one could enter without leaving traces behind. Two weeks later the seals were broken and the room opened; the wheel was still revolving. The door was resealed, and this time it remained closed until 4 January 1718. The wheel was still revolving at twenty-six revolutions per minute.

Deeply impressed, his doubts now laid at rest, the Landgrave asked Orffyreus how much he wanted for his secret and turned pale when Orrifyreus replied, "Twenty thousand pounds." It was his greatest invention and his life's work, he reminded them, and he deserved adequate compensation. The Landgrave and his retinue of scientists was inclined to agree, but he didn't have that much money to hand. Baron Fischer, architect to the Emperor of Austria, pointed out that it should be easy to raise the money in London, and accordingly wrote to Dr J. T. Desaguliers of the Royal Society. The arrangement he proposed was that if the movement of the wheel should prove to be "a perpetual one", then the £20,000 should be given to the inventor; if not, the money would be returned.

Meanwhile Professor Gravesande had made a thorough examination of the axle of the machine, and wrote a report to the effect that as far as he could see there was no way in which the wheel could be a fake. Unfortunately, the paranoid inventor suspected that Gravesande was asked to examine the axle in the hope of discovering the secret without paying for it. Orffyreus exploded. He locked himself in the room, and smashed the wheel. Then he wrote a message on the wall, declaring that it was the impertinent curiosity of Gravesande that had provoked him.

And now, regrettably, Orffyreus and his machine vanish into obscurity. If Orffyreus had lived a century later he would have been pursued by prying journalists, and we would have a detailed history of the rest of his life. But these were the days before the invention of newspapers, and all we know is that Orffyreus was rebuilding his machine ten years later, in 1727, and that Gravesande had agreed to examine it again. But there is no record that it was ever tested. All we know is that Orffyreus died in 1745, at the age of sixty-five. And his secret, whatever it was, died with him.

The mystery here is surely psychological rather than scientific. If we accept that energy cannot be created or destroyed, then we must conclude that the wheel was a fraud, no matter how well its inventor succeeded in concealing it. Orffyreus, according to one contemporary, had been a clockmaker at some point, and we must assume that he had found some method of concealing a spring mechanism somewhere in the supports. We may assume that other explanations such as that a man was concealed inside it are ruled out by the crucial test in which the machine was left in a locked room for three months.

Yet if we assume that Orffyreus was a fraud, the puzzle remains. What could he hope to gain from it? There was no way in which he could have absconded with the £20,000, for as we can see from Baron Fischer's letter, the money would not even be handed over unless they were first satisfied that he had genuinely discovered the principle of perpetual motion.

It must also be admitted that Orffyreus's character makes it seem unlikely that he was a straightforward swindler. Charm and smoothness are an essential part of the equipment of the confidence man; and while there is no guarantee

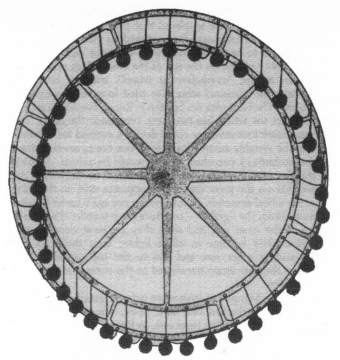

Rupert Gould's drawing of the "overbalancing wheel".

that paranoia and bad temper are a sign of genius, there is no denying that we find it hard to associate such characteristics with a deliberate confidence trickster. They are more likely to be accompanied by a certain obsessive quality, a conviction of one's own remarkable talents. It is easier to believe that Orffyreus was a self-deceiver than that he was a crook. But could a self-deceiver construct a wheel that would run for three months in a locked room?

On the other hand, let us suppose that Orffyreus was a man with a grudge – a man who was quite certain about his own genius, but who resented his lack of recognition. It *is* conceivable that in a mood of rage and contempt he decided to practise a deliberate swindle, and then use the money to devote the rest of his life to his researches. How could he hope to carry out such a swindle?

A careful study of the case suggests some possible answers. Orffyreus himself published a pamphlet, typically entitled *The Triumphant Orffyrean Perpetual Motion* (1719), in which he offers an exceedingly obscure account of his basic principles. He admits that his wheel depends upon weights, which "constitute the perpetual motion itself, since from them is received the universal movement which they must exercise so long as they remain out of the centre of gravity". These weights, he says, are so placed that they can "never obtain equilibrium". Professors who examined his machine described being able to hear the movements of about eight weights, presumably placed on the rim of the wheel. This principle is known as the "overbalancing wheel", and has been the mainstay of inventors who have tried to produce perpetual motion. The basic idea can be seen in Rupert Gould's drawing. If in fact the wheel has two rims, one inside the other, and some ingenious inventor could devise a method for transferring the weights automatically from one rim to another, then the problem of perpetual motion would be solved. As they transfer to the outer rim, they cause it to outweigh the weights on the inner rim on the opposite side, so that side of the wheel descends. As it begins to rise again under its own momentum the "grabs" – or whatever – transfer the weight on to the inner rim, and since they are now closer to the centre, they become in effect lighter than those on the descending outer rim, and rise to the top of the wheel, where they are again transferred to the outer rim. It sounds foolproof.

But the Marquis of Worcester (who originally thought of the idea) overlooked one basic point. The outer rim is of course longer than the inner one, so there are less weights on the descending rim than on the other side. (In Gould's drawing, it can be seen that there are twenty weights on one side of the wheel compared to eighteen on the other.) So the two sides exactly counterbalance one another, and the wheel soon comes to a halt.

But this is not a point that would immediately strike anybody who studied a drawing or model of the over-balancing wheel. And it is conceivable that Orffyreus may have reckoned on this in deceiving the Landgrave and his wise men. We may suppose that he secreted some kind of powerful clock-spring inside the supports of his machine, with a cogwheel that turned the axle. When the time came to hand over his secret he would remove the canvas cover of the wheel and reveal his ingeniously designed "overbalancing wheel". And unless the savants were extremely astute, or had given long consideration to the problem, they would agree that Orffyreus had indeed solved the problem of perpetual motion in an absurdly simple way. And by the time they dismantled the wheel and found the clock-spring mechanism, Orffyreus would be a hundred miles away.

But there is also an objection to this explanation. It is easy to design a modern clock or watch that will run for a year, because the "moving parts" are so light that they can be driven by a tiny battery. But a twelve-foot wheel with weights round the rim would require a great deal more energy: a heavy-duty car battery might do it, but a clock-spring that would drive such a wheel for two months would have to be enormous. There is no obvious room inside Orffyreus's wheel for such a spring. And unless Orffyreus had invented the principle of the dynamo a century and a half before Faraday, there seems to be no other possibility. And so we are left once more with the tantalizing possibility that perhaps Orffyreus *did* stumble upon some simple but profound secret that has eluded all his successors.

Latvian Edward Leedskalnin built his house out of local Florida stone. This stone is a very hard and dense form of coral. Leedskalnin worked without modern tools, using mainly timber and scrap metal to quarry and move the blocks of masonry he used, some of which weighed over thirty tons. Not only did he build a house totally without help, he also quarried twelve stone rocking-chairs, finely balanced upon their curved bases. He built stone astronomical instruments and a stone map of Florida. The door to his stone park was a nine-ton coral slab so finely poised upon its centre of gravity that it could be swung backwards and forwards at the touch of a finger.

He eventually decided to move all of his objects to a more accessible site and open a children's playground. He hired a lorry and moved it all himself. No one knows how the slight four-foot eight man achieved all this on his own. No one saw him move the objects, but move they did. Enquiries into Leedskalnin's secret brought a knowing look and oblique statements about having rediscovered the methods of the ancient pyramid architects.

He died in 1951, never having revealed his method.

Chapter Twelve

Psychometry, "Telescope into the Past"

In the winter of 1921 members of the Metapsychic Institute in Paris met together to test a clairvoyant. Someone produced a letter and asked someone to pass it to her; before it could reach her it was grabbed by a novelist called Pascal Fortunny, who said scathingly: "It can't be difficult to invent something that applies to anybody." He then closed his eyes and pronounced solemnly: "Ah yes, I see a crime, a murder . . ." When he had finished the man who had brought the letter said: "That was written by Henri Landru." Landru was the "Bluebeard" who was then on trial for the murders of eleven women. The sceptic Fortunny had discovered that he possessed the curious ability known as psychometry – the ability to "sense" the history of an object by holding it in the hand.

According to the man who invented the word – an American doctor named Joseph Rodes Buchanan – it is an ability we all possess, although most of us have unconsciously suppressed it. Buchanan – who was a professor of medicine in Kentucky – came to suspect the existence of such a faculty in 1841, when he met a bishop named Leonidas Polk, who claimed that he could always detect brass when he touched it – even in the dark – because it produced a peculiar taste in his mouth. Buchanan was interested in the science known as phrenology – the notion that the "bumps" on our skulls reveal our characters – and he was interested to discover that Polk seemed to have a highly developed "bump" of sensibility. So he decided to perform a scientific test on students who had a similar bump. Various metals were wrapped in paper, and Buchanan was delighted to discover that many of his students could detect brass, iron, lead and so on by merely pressing their fingertips against the paper. They could also distinguish substances like salt, sugar, pepper and vinegar.

Buchanan concluded that the answer lay in some "nerve aura" in the fingertips, which can detect different metals exactly as we could distinguish them by touching them with the tip of the tongue. This appeared to be confirmed by his observation that it seemed to work better when the hands are damp with perspiration – for after all a damp skin is more "sensitive" than a dry skin. But this explanation began to seem inadequate when he discovered that one of his best "sensitives" – a man named Charles Inman – could sense the contents of sealed letters, and the character of the writers. Buchanan's explanation was that the "nerve aura" of the writer had left some kind of trace on the letter, and Inman was able to pick up this trace through his own nerve aura. In other words, Inman's "sensitivity" was abnormally developed, in much the same way as a bloodhound's sense of smell. But that theory also broke down when he discovered that Inman displayed the same insight when presented with photographs – daguerreotypes – in sealed envelopes. Even the argument that the photograph had been in contact with the "sitter", and had therefore picked up something of his "nerve aura", ceased to be convincing when Buchanan discovered that newspaper photographs worked as well as daguerreotypes.

The professor of geology at Boston University, William Denton, read Buchanan's original paper on psychometry – the word means "soul measurement" – and decided to try it himself. His sister Anne was "highly impressible", and she proved to be an even better psychometrist than Inman; she was not only able to describe the character of letter-writers; she was even able to describe their physical appearance and surroundings.

This led Denton to ask himself whether, if a writer's image and surroundings could be "impressed" on a letter, "why could not rocks receive impressions of surrounding objects, some of which they have been in the immediate neighbourhood of for years"? So in 1853 Denton began testing his "sensitives" with geological and archaeological specimens, "and was delighted to find that without possessing any previous knowledge of the specimen, or even seeing it, the history of its time passed before the gaze of the seer like a grand panoramic view". When he handed his sister a piece of volcanic lava from Hawaii, she was shaken to see "an ocean of fire pouring over a precipice and boiling as it pours". Significantly, she also saw the sea with ships on it, and Denton knew that the lava had been ejected during an eruption in 1840, when the American navy had been in Hawaii. A fragment of bone found in a piece of limestone evoked a picture of a prehistoric beach with dinosaurs. A fragment of Indian pottery brought a vision of Red Indians. A meteorite fragment brought visions of empty space, with the stars looking abnormally large and bright. A fragment of rock from Niagara brought a vision of a boiling torrent hurling up spray (which she thought was steam). A piece of stalactite brought an image of pieces of rock hanging down like icicles. To make doubly sure that his sensitives were not somehow picking up unconscious hints or recognizing the specimens, Denton wrapped them in thick paper. He also discovered that when he tried the same specimen a second time – perhaps a month later – it produced the same result, although the picture was never identical.

In one of his most interesting experiments he showed his wife a fragment of Roman tile which came from a villa that had belonged to the orator Cicero. She described a Roman villa and lines of soldiers; she also saw the owner of the villa, a genial, fleshy man with an air of command. Denton was disappointed; Cicero had been tall and thin. But by the time Denton came to write the second volume of *The Soul of*

Things, he had discovered that the villa had also belonged to the dictator Sulla, and that Sulla *did* fit his wife's description.

Another impressive "hit" was the "vision" induced by a piece of volcanic rock from Pompeii. Mrs Denton had no idea what it was, and was not allowed to see it; but she had a vivid impression of the eruption of Vesuvius and the crowds fleeing from Pompeii. Denton's son Sherman had an even more detailed vision of ancient Pompeii, complete with many archaeological details – such as an image of a boat with a "swan's neck" which proved to be historically accurate.

Denton was immensely excited; he believed that he and Buchanan had discovered a so far unknown human faculty, a kind of "telescope into the past" that would enable us to relive great scenes of history. In effect, everything that had ever happened to the world was preserved on a kind of "newsreel" (although this was not, of course, an image that occurred to Denton) and could be replayed at will.

But while the evidence for the psychometric faculty is undoubtedly beyond dispute, Denton was not aware of how far it can be deceptive. The third volume of *The Soul of Things,* published in 1888, contains "visions" of various planets that we now know to be preposterous. Venus has giant trees like toadstools and animals that sound as if they were invented by Hieronymus Bosch; Mars has a summery temperature (in fact it would be freezing) and is peopled with four-fingered men with blue eyes and yellow hair; Jupiter also has blue-eyed blondes with plaits down to their waists and the ability to float like balloons. Denton's son Sherman (who was responsible for most of these extraordinary descriptions) had clearly developed the faculty that Jung calls "active imagination", and was unable to distinguish it from his genuine psychometric abilities.

What impresses the modern reader about Denton's *Soul of Things* and Buchanan's *Manual of Psychometry* (optimistically sub-titled The Dawn of a New Civilization), is their thoroughly scientific approach. This also impressed their contemporaries at first. Unfortunately, the period when they were conducting their experiments was also the period when the new craze known as Spiritualism was spreading across America and Europe. It had started with curious poltergeist manifestations in the home of the Fox family in New York state in the late 1840s. By 1860 it was a worldwide phenomenon. Scientists were appalled, and most of them dismissed it as sheer delusion. Anything that seemed remotely connected with the "supernatural" became the object of the same scepticism, and the researches of Buchanan and Denton never attracted the attention they deserved. Denton died in 1883, Buchanan in 1900, both in relative obscurity.

The next major experiments in psychometry were made by Dr Gustav Pagenstecher, a German who moved to Mexico City in the 1880s, and who regarded himself as a hard-headed materialist. Some time after World War I, Pagenstecher was treating the insomnia of a patient called Maria Reyes de Zierold by hypnosis. One day, as she lay in a hypnotic trance, she told him that her daughter was listening at the door. Pagenstecher opened the door and found the daughter there. He began testing Maria for paranormal abilities and discovered that while under hypnosis she could share his own sensations; if he put sugar or salt on his tongue; she could taste it; if he held a lighted match near his fingers she felt the heat of the flame. Then he began testing her for psychometric abilities. Like Denton's subjects, she could describe where some specimen came from. Holding a sea-shell, she described an underwater scene; holding a piece of meteorite, she described hurtling through space and down through the earth's atmosphere. ("I am horrified! My God!") Dr Walter Franklin Prince, who tested her on behalf of the American Society for Psychical Research, handed her what he thought was a "sea bean" which he had found on the beach. She described a tropical forest. Professional botanists confirmed that the "bean" was a nut from a tree that grew in

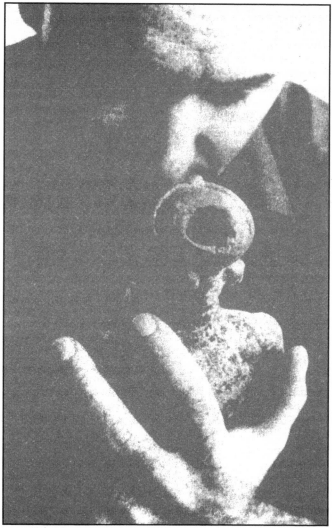

Psychic Peter Nelson, USA, performing psychometry
experiment, 1984. *Dr Elmar Gruber/Fortean Picture Library*

the tropical forest, and that was often carried down to the sea by the rivers.

Another eminent experimenter of the 1920s was Dr Eugene Osty, director of the Metapsychical Institute at which the novelist Pascal Fortunny correctly identified the letter from the mass murderer Landru. In his classic work *Supernormal Faculties in Man*, Osty described many experiments in psychometry with various "sensitives". In 1921 he was handed a photograph of a sealed glass capsule containing some liquid; it had been found near the great temple at Baalbek. One of his best psychics, a Mme Moral, held the photograph in her hand – it was so blurred it could have been of anything – and said immediately that it reminded her of "a place with dead people", and of one old man in particular. She "saw" a vast place, like an enormous church, then went on to describe the man, who was obviously a high priest. The capsule in the photograph contained the blood of a man who had been sacrificed in some distant land, and had been placed in the priest's grave as a memento.

At the time Osty himself had no idea what the photograph represented, and was surprised when the engineer who had found it was able to confirm that it had been discovered in a rich tomb in the Bekaa valley.

This story raises again the central problem about psychometry. Buchanan's original hypothesis – that it was simply a matter of "nerve aura", so the psychometrist could be regarded as a kind of human bloodhound – ceases to be plausible if the information can be picked up from a photograph, which could not be expected to retain any kind of "scent". Even Denton's assumption that every object somehow "photographs" its surroundings seems dubious. In that case a piece of Roman pavement could only have "photographed" a limited area, and Mrs Denton's view of Roman legionaries would have been simply of hairy legs towering up above her.

The likeliest hypothesis is that the faculty involved is what is traditionally known as "clairvoyance", a peculiar ability to "know" what is going on in some other place or at some other time. But Bishop Polk's ability to distinguish brass in the dark is obviously not clairvoyance. Here, as in so many other areas of the "paranormal", it is practically impossible to draw neat dividing lines.

Many modern psychometrists – like Gerard Croiset, Peter Hurkos and Suzanne Padfield – have been able use their faculty to help the police solve crimes: Suzanne Padfield was even able to help the Moscow police catch a child-murderer without leaving her home in Dorset.[1] But it is significant that Croiset disliked being called a psychometrist or clairvoyant, and preferred the more ambiguous word "paragnost" – meaning simply the ability to "know" what lies beyond the normal limits of the senses.

1. See *The Psychic Detectives* by Colin Wilson.

Archaeologists in Iraq have found what appears to be an ancient electric battery. The object, dating from roughly 230 **BC**, was found in an excavation of a Parthian village in 1936. It consists of a small vase containing a copper cylinder surrounding an iron rod. Sceptics insist that it is a scroll case. However it cannot be denied that if an acid such as lemon juice is poured into such a vase, an electric current is created. In fact the current is sufficient to be used to electroplate metal objects suspended in the correct metal solution.

If the battery was indeed used for this purpose it may mean that much of what modern museums classify as ancient gold may only be plate . . .

Chapter Thirteen

Did Robin Hood Really Exist?

Next to King Arthur, Robin Hood is the most famous of British heroes, and he shares with King Arthur the indignity of having his existence doubted by modern scholarship. The folklorist Lord Raglan conduded that he was really a Celtic god, while in *The God of the Witches* Margaret Murray argues that his name means *"Robin of the Hood"*, and that he was probably the devil (or horned god) in ancient witchcraft festivals. Yet there is also convincing evidence that Robin was a real person, and that – as the ballads declare – he plundered the king's deer in Sherwood Forest and had a long-standing feud with the Sheriff of Nottingham.

The first literary reference to Robin Hood occurs in William Langland's *Piers Plowman*, dating from around 1377. Langland makes a priest remark that he could not say his paternoster without making mistakes, but "I know rhymes of Robyn Hood and Randolf Earl of Chester". So there were already ballads of Robin Hood by that date. In 1510 Wynkyn de Worde, one of the earliest printers, brought out *A Lytell Geste of Robyn Hood*, which did for Robin Hood what Malory had done for King Arthur in the middle of the previous century. And by the time he appears in Sir Walter Scott's *Ivanhoe* (1847), Robin had become the boon-companion and ally of Richard the Lion Heart, the heroic outlaw of the woods. All that was needed then was for some folklorist to notice how often Robin Hood's name is associated with folk festivals, like the

Little John's Grave, Hathersage churchyard, Derbyshire.
Fortean Picture Library.

Hobby Horse ceremony which takes place on May Day in Padstow, Cornwall,[1] to suggest that Robin Hood was really Robin Wood, and that his name is derived from the Norse god Woden . . . In fact he appears as Robin Wood in T. H. White's *Sword in the Stone*, in which he becomes a contemporary of King Arthur, who (if he ever existed) was said to have died about AD 540.

Those who assume there is no smoke without fire are inclined to believe that Robin Hood was a real outlaw who at some time lived in Sherwood Forest, and who became so popular during his own lifetime that, like Billy the Kid, he soon became the subject of tales and ballads. Yet it seems unlikely that he was around as early as Richard the Lion Heart (1157–99), or he would surely have been mentioned in manuscripts before *Piers Plowman* two centuries later. In his *Chronicle of Scotland*, written about 1420, Andrew Wyntoun refers to Robin Hood and Little John for the year 1283, which sounds altogether more likely – about a century before *Piers Plowman*.

And where precisely did he operate? One important clue is that there is a small fishing town called Robin Hood's Bay in Yorkshire, not far from Whitby, and that up on the nearby moors there are two tumuli (or barrows) called Robin Hood's Butts. Another is that in medieval England the forest of Barnsdale in Yorkshire joined Sherwood Forest in Nottinghamshire. A sixteenth-century life of Robin Hood among the Sloane Manuscripts says he was born in Locksley, in Yorkshire, about 1160. The *Chronicle of Scotland* associates Robin with "Barnysale" presumably Barnsdale. So the evidence suggests that he was a Yorkshireman.

Later legends declare that he was "Sir Robin of Locksley", or even the Earl of Huntingdon. But it is clear from the earlier ballads that he was a yeoman – a farmer who owns his own land – and that this is partly why he became such a hero: not

---

1. Actually 8 May, but the date has become displaced over the centuries.

because he was a nobleman, but because he was a representative of the people. (A small tenant farmer would be only one stage above a landless peasant.)

One of the most important clues to Robin's identity emerged in the mid-nineteenth century, when the Historic Documents Commission was cataloguing thousands of documents which represented eight centuries of British history. It was in 1852 that the antiquary Joseph Hunter claimed that he had stumbled upon a man who sounded as if he might be the original Robin Hood. His name in fact was Robert, and he was the son of Adam Hood, a forester in the service of the Earl de Warenne. (Robin was simply a diminutive of Robert – not, in those days, a name in its own right.) He was born about 1280, and on 25 January 1316 Robert Hood and his wife Matilda paid two shillings for permission to take a piece of the earl's waste ground in "Bickhill" (or Bitch-hill) in Wakefield. It was merely the size of a kitchen garden – thirty feet long by sixteen feet wide. The rent for this was sixpence a year. The Manor Court Roll for 1357 shows a house "formerly the property of Robert Hode" on the site – so by that time Robert Hood was presumably dead.

Now, 1316 was midway through the reign of Edward II, the foppish, homosexual king who was finally murdered – by having a red-hot spit inserted into his entrails – in September 1327. After his coronation (in 1307) he dismissed his father's ministers and judges and made his lover, Piers Gaveston, Earl of Cornwall – to the fury of his barons. It was the most powerful of these, Thomas, Earl of Lancaster, who forced Edward to accept the rule of twenty-eight barons (called Ordainers), and who finally executed Piers Gaveston in 1312. Edward's lack of attention to affairs of state allowed the Scots – against whom his father Edward I had fought so successfully – to throw off their English masters. Edward II was defeated at Bannockburn in 1314, two years before Robert Hood hired the piece of waste ground and set up home with his wife Matilda. So it is understandable that when the Earl of Warenne was ordered by the king to raise a troop to fight the Scots, Robert Hood failed to oblige, and the records show that he was accordingly fined. But when a second muster was raised in 1317 Hood's name was not listed among those fined – which led J. W. Walker, a modern historian, to conclude that this time Robert Hood joined the army. Five years later it was the Earl of Lancaster who raised the army, to fight against the king. Again, Hood's name is not among those fined, so it again seems that he answered the summons. Lancaster's army was defeated at Boroughbridge, and Lancaster was captured and beheaded. The quarrel had been about Edward's new favourites, the Despensers, father and son, whom he had been forced to banish; now he was able to recall them.

Many of Lancaster's supporters were declared outlaws, and Walker discovered a document that stated that a "building of five rooms" on Bickhill, Wakefield, was among the property confiscated. Walker believes that this was Robert Hood's home, and that the outlaw now took refuge in the nearby forest of Barnsdale, where he soon became a highly successful robber.

Now, it must be understood that if Robert Hood *was* the legendary Robin, and he took refuge in the forest, living off the deer population, he was risking horrible penalties. When William the Conqueror brought the Normans to England he declared that the forests – which covered a third of the land – were his own property; any peasant who killed deer risked literally being flayed alive. Under William, the Saxons suffered as much as countries occupied by the Nazis in World War II. Two and a half centuries later the Normans regarded themselves as Englishmen, and the French language had ceased to be used in England, but the laws were still harsh. The "forest laws" had been mitigated, so a man could no longer have his hands or his lips sliced off for poaching a deer; but the penalty was still a heavy fine, a year's imprisonment, and sureties for his future good behaviour. If he could not find guarantors he had to "abjure the realm" – quit the kingdom for ever.

The battle of Boroughbridge was fought on 16 March 1322, near the Ure river in Yorkshire; dismounted men-at-arms and archers drove back the cavalry, then another royalist army moved up behind the rebels and forced them to surrender. Lancaster was captured and tried; evidence revealed that he had been contemplating an alliance with the king's old enemy, Robert the Bruce. Lancaster – the king's cousin – was beheaded. And Robin Hood, deprived of his home, became an outlaw in the king's forest.

But if Walker is correct in identifying Robert Hood of Wakefield as Robin Hood, he was not an outlaw for long. In the spring of the following year the king made a progress through the north of England, reaching York on 1 May. From 16 May to 21 May he stayed at Rothwell, between Wakefield and Leeds, and spent three days hunting at Plumpton Park in Knaresborough Forest. And the *Lytell Geste* makes this visit a part of the story of Robin Hood, describing how the king "came to Plumpton Park/ And failed [missed] many of his deer". Where the king was accustomed to seeing herds of deer, now he could find only one deer "that bore any good horn". Which made the king swear by the Trinity "I wish I could lay my hands on Robin Hood":

> I wolde I had Robyn Hode
> With eyen I myght hym se.

So, according to this ballad, one of the foresters suggested that the king should disguise himself as an abbot, riding through the greenwood with a band of monks. The ruse was successful; Robin and his men stopped the "abbot", but recognized him as the king. And the king thereupon found Robin so likeable that he invited him to join the royal household as a *vadlet*, a gentleman of the royal bedchamber. The king continued on his travels until February 1324, when he returned to Westminster. The royal household accounts for April record payment of the past month's wages to Robyn Hod and twenty-eight others. The first record of a payment to Robyn Hod is in the previous June. The ballad tells us that after being a servant of the king for somewhat over a year, Robin asked the king's permission to return to Barnsdale. And the household accounts for November 1324 record that Robyn Hod, formerly one of the "porteurs" (gentlemen of the bedchamber) had been given five shillings "because he is no longer able to work". The ballad says that Robin asked the king's leave to return to Barnsdale, and was given permission to stay for seven days. But he never returned; instead he regrouped his merry men, and lived on in the greenwood for another twenty-two years. If this is based on fact, then he died about 1346, in his mid-sixties.

The king's fortunes took a downward turn after Robin's departure. He had recalled the banished Despensers, and the younger of the two had become his "favourite" to the disgust of his queen, who had already had to contend with Piers Gaveston. She was a Frenchwoman, daughter of Philip the Fair. Now she began to take a romantic interest in an unpleasant and ambitious young baron called Roger de Mortimer, who had been thrown into the Tower for his opposition to the Despensers. Queen Isabella became his mistress, and it was probably she who plotted Mortimer's escape. He fled to Paris and was joined there by Isabella, who was on a mission for the king. They landed at Orwell, in Suffolk, with an army of almost three thousand. When the king heard the news he fled, and was captured, and imprisoned in Berkeley Castle. He was forced to abdicate, and his son (aged fifteen) was crowned Edward III. On the night of 21 September 1327 horrible screams rang through the castle. The next morning it was announced that the king had died "of natural causes". There were no marks on the body, but it is said that his features were still contorted with agony. A chronicle of some thirty years later states that three assassins entered his cell when he was asleep, and held down the upper half of his body with a table. Then a horn was inserted into the anal orifice, and a red-hot iron bar was used to burn out the king's insides.

Mortimer and Isabella ruled England as regents for four years; then the young king asserted himself, had Mortimer seized in Nottingham Castle, and had him executed as a traitor at Tyburn. The loss of her lover almost drove the queen mad. But she was restored to favour, and lived on for another twenty-eight years.

It is of course conceivable that the Robin Hood who lived in Edward's reign had no connection with the legendary outlaw of Sherwood Forest; one reference book (*Who's Who In History*) says that he was alive in 1230, in the reign of Henry III, on the grounds that records show that the Sheriff of Yorkshire sold his possessions in that year (for 32*s* 6*d*) when he became an outlaw; but the same reference book admits that the Robyn Hode of Wakefield is also a good contender. There is something to be said for this earlier dating, for it would give more time for the legend of Robin Hood to spread throughout England. But there is also a great deal to be said for Robin Hood of Wakefield. If he became an outlaw in 1322, as a result of the Lancaster rebellion, then he spent only one year in Sherwood Forest before the king pardoned him. The story of his pardon by the homosexual king certainly rings true – as does his appointment as a gentleman of the bedchamber. It is natural to speculate that he may have found that his duties in the bedchamber involved more than he had bargained for, although at this time the king's favourite was the younger Hugh le Despenser (executed by Mortimer and Isabella in 1326). So he returned to the greenwood, and became a hero of legend. We do not know whether he became the arch-enemy of the Sheriff of Nottingham, but the sheriff – who would be the equivalent of a modern Chief Constable – would have been responsible for law and order in Nottinghamshire and south Yorkshire, and would certainly have resented a band of outlaws who lived off the king's deer. One chronicle states that Robin also had a retreat in what became known as Robin Hood's Bay, and ships in which he could escape to sea. (He is also said to have operated as far afield as Cumberland.) If a concerted attempt had been made to flush him out, it would probably have succeeded. But most of the peasants and tenant farmers would have been on Robin's side. There had been a time when the forests of England were common land, and half-starved peasantry must have felt it was highly unreasonable that thousands of square miles of forest should be reserved for the king's hunting, when the king could not make use of a fraction of that area.

But there could be another reason that Robin was allowed to operate without too much opposition. When he was at court he must surely have met the fourteen-year-old boy who would become Edward III, and Edward would be of exactly the right age to look with admiration on a famous outlaw. This is only speculation, but it could undoubtedly explain why Robin was allowed to become the legendary bane of authority in the last decades of his life.

Authority has its own ways of striking back. According to the Sloane Manuscript, Robin fell ill, and went to his cousin, the Prioress of Kirklees; to be bled – the standard procedure for treating any illness in those days. She decided to avenge the many churchmen he had robbed, and allowed him to bleed to death. Another account says that she betrayed him at the request of her lover, Sir Roger de Doncaster. Still another source states that the man responsible for Robin's death was a monk who was called in to attend him, and who decided that the outlaw would be better dead. He was buried in the grounds of the nunnery, within a bowshot of its walls. Grafton's Chronicle (1562) says he was buried under an inscribed stone, and a century later another chronicle reported that his tomb, with a plain cross on a flat stone, could be seen in the cemetery; in 1665 Dr Nathaniel Johnstone made a drawing of it; Gough's *Sepulchral Monuments* also has an engraving of the tombstone. In the early nineteenth century navvies building a railway broke up the stone – it is said they believed its chips to be a cure for toothache. So the last trace of the real existence of Robin Hood disappeared. But by that time the grave of the prioress had been discovered among the ruins of the nunnery and it bore some resemblance to the tomb of Robin Hood. It also mentioned her name – Elizabeth Stainton.

The real significance of Robin Hood is that he lived in a century when the peasants were beginning to feel an increasing resentment about their condition – a resentment that expressed itself in the revolutionary doctrines of John Ball and which exploded in the Peasants' Revolt of 1381, only a short time after Robin is first mentioned in print by Langland. The Peasants' Revolt is generally considered to mark the end of the Middle Ages; but it is in the ballads of Robin Hood that we can see that the state of mind known as the Middle Ages is coming to an end.

Chapter Fourteen

Synchronicity or "Mere Coincidence"?

The *Sunday Times* journalist Godfrey Smith was thinking of writing something about the "saga of lost manuscripts" – Carlyle's manuscript of The *French Revolution*, burnt by a careless maid, T. E. Lawrence's *Seven Pillars of Wisdom*, left in a taxi, Hemingway's suitcase full of early manuscripts, stolen from a train – and decided to call on the literary agent Hilary Rubinstein, a treasure-house of similar stories. But before he could introduce the subject into the conversation a girl sitting with them – the wife of the novelist Nicholas Mosley – mentioned that her husband was upset because he had just had the first 150 pages of his new novel stolen from his car. Smith remarked in his *Sunday Times* column: "we are back in what J. W. Dunne called serial time, and Arthur Koestler called synchronicity, and some of us still call coincidence . . ."

It was Jung in fact who coined the word "synchronicity" for meaningful coincidence. But Arthur Koestler was equally intrigued by the subject, and discussed it in a book called *The Roots of Coincidence* in 1972. In the following year he wrote an article about coincidence in the *Sunday Times* and appealed to readers for examples. Many of these were utilized in his book *The Challenge of Chance* (1973), co-authored by Sir Alister Hardy and Robert Harvie. He begins with a section called "The Library Angel", describing coincidences involved with books. In 1972 Koestler had been asked to write about the chess championship between Boris Spassky and Bobbie Fischer, so he went to the London Library to look up books on chess and books on Iceland. He decided to start with chess and the first book that caught his eye was entitled *Chess in Iceland* by Williard Fiske.

He then tells of how Dame Rebecca West was trying to check up on an episode related by one of the accused in one of the Nuremberg war-crimes trials, and how she discovered to her annoyance that the trials are published in the form of abstracts under arbitrary headings and are therefore useless to a researcher. After an hour of fruitless searching she approached a librarian and said: "I can't find it . . .", and casually took a volume off the shelf and opened it. It opened at the page she had been searching for.

This anecdote is particularly interesting because it involved an apparently "random" action, a casual reaching out without logical purpose. The word "synchronicity" was coined by Jung in connection with the *I Ching,* the Chinese *Book of Changes*, which the Chinese consult as an "oracle". The method of "consulting" the *I Ching* consists of throwing down three coins at random half a dozen times and noting whether there are more heads or tails. Two or three tails gives a line with a break in the middle, thus: three heads gives an unbroken line. The six lines, placed on top of one another, form a "hexagram":

The above hexagram is number 58, "The Joyous – Lake", with a "Judgement:": "The Joyous, Success – Perseverance is favourable". But from the logical point of view it is obviously impossible to explain how throwing down coins at random can provide an answer – even if the question has been very clearly and precisely formulated in the mind before the coins are thrown.

The experience of Rebecca West can provide a glimmering of an answer. She was looking for a particular passage. We may assume that some unconscious faculty of "extra-sensory perception" guided her to the right place before she began to speak to the librarian, and then guided her hand as she casually reached out. But could it also cause the book to open in the right place? This would seem to require something more than "ESP", something for which Horace Walpole coined the word "serendipity", "the faculty of making happy and unexpected discoveries by chance". And what of the "chance" that caused the librarian to be standing in the right place at that moment? We have here such a complex situation that it is difficult to conceive of some purely "passive" faculty – a kind of intuition – capable of accounting for it. Unless we wish to fall back on "coincidence", we have to think in terms of some faculty capable to some extent of "engineering" a situation as well as merely taking advantage of it. And the use of the *I Ching* also seems to presuppose the use of such a faculty in causing the coins to fall in a certain order.

For most of his life Jung was unwilling even to conceive of such a possibility – at least publicly. (He was, in fact, using the *I Ching* as an oracle from the early 1920s.)

In 1944, when he was sixty-eight years old, Jung slipped on an icy road and broke his ankle; this led to a severe heart attack. While hovering between life and death, Jung experienced curious visions, in one of which he was hovering above the earth, out in space, then saw a kind of Hindu temple inside a meteor. "Night after night I floated in a state of purest bliss." He was convinced that if he recovered his doctor would have to die – and in fact the doctor died as Jung started to recover. The result of these strange experiences was that Jung ceased to be concerned about whether his contemporaries regarded him as a mystic rather than a

scientist, and he ceased to make a secret of his lifelong
interest in "the occult". In 1949 he wrote his influential introduction to Richard Wilhelm's edition of the *I Ching*, in which
he speaks about the "acausal connecting principle" called
synchronicity; in the following year he wrote his paper *On
Synchronicity*, later expanded into a book. Unfortunately,
Jung's fundamental premise in both these seminal works is
basically nonsensical. Western science, he says, is based on
the principle of causality. But modern physics is shaking this
principle to its foundations; we now know that natural laws
are merely statistical truths, and that therefore we must
allow for exceptions. This is, of course, untrue. The
philosopher Hume had argued that causality is not a basic
law of the universe; a pan of water usually boils when we put
it on a fire, but it *might* freeze. Kant later used this argument
to demonstrate that the stuff of the universe is basically
"mental". We can now see that these arguments were
fallacious. It is true that a pan of water might freeze when
placed on a fire, if the atmospheric pressure were suddenly
increased a thousandfold. But this would not be a defiance of
the law of causality, merely a change in some of the basic
conditions of the experiment. And by the same argument, we
can see that modern physics has *not* demonstrated that the
laws of nature are "statistical", and that once in a billion
times they might be "broken". A law of nature cannot be
broken except for some very good "legal" reason.

So Jung's talk about an "acausal connecting principle"
may be dismissed as verbal mystification, designed to throw
dust in the eyes of scientists who would otherwise accuse
him of becoming superstitious in his old age. The example
Jung gives of synchronicity makes this clear. He tells how, on
1 April 1949, they had fish for lunch, and someone
mentioned the custom of making an "April fish" (i.e. April
fool) of someone. In the afternoon a patient showed him
pictures of fish which she had painted. In the evening he was
shown a piece of embroidery with fish-like monsters on it.

Synchronicity or "Mere Coincidence"?

The next morning another patient told him a dream of a fish. At this time Jung was studying the fish symbol in history, and before this string of coincidences began had made a note of a Latin quotation about fish. It is, says Jung, very natural to feel that this is a case of "meaningful coincidence" – i.e. that there is an "acausal connection". But if the coincidence is "meaningful", then there must be a causal connection – even if (as Jung is implying) it is not one that would be recognized by science. Jung is in fact suggesting that there is some hidden connection between the mind and nature.

Jung was not the first to consider this possibility. The Austrian biologist Paul Kammerer – who committed suicide after being accused of faking some of his experiments – was fascinated by odd coincidences, and wrote a book, *The Law of Series*, about it. The book contains a hundred samples of coincidence. For example, in 1915 his wife was reading about a character called Mrs Rohan in a novel; on the tram soon after she saw a man who resembled her friend Prince Rohan; that evening Prince Rohan dropped in to see them. In the tram she had heard someone ask the man who looked like Rohan whether he knew the village of Weissenbach on Lake Attersee; when she got off the tram she walked into a delicatessen shop, and the assistant asked her if she knew Weissenbach on Lake Attersee . . .

Kammerer's theory was that events *do* happen in "clusters", which are natural but not "causal". He thought of it as some unknown mathematical law – a "law of seriality". In short, "absurd" coincidences *are* a law of nature. He spent his days carefully noting all kinds of things – the age, sex and dress of people walking past him in a park or sitting on a tram – and observed the typical "clustering".

Jung offers one of the most amusing examples of "clustering" in his book on synchronicity – it was originally told by the scientist Camille Flammarion in his book *The Unknown*. The poet Emile Deschamps was given a piece of plum pudding by a certain M. Fortgibu when he was at boarding-school – the dish was then almost unknown in France, but Fortgibu had just returned from England. Ten years later Deschamps saw plum pudding in the window of a Paris restaurant and went in to ask if he could have some. He was told that unfortunately the pudding had been ordered by someone else – M. Fortgibu, who was sitting there, and who offered to share it. Years later he attended a party at which there was to be plum pudding, and he told the story about M. Fortgibu. As they sat eating plum pudding the door opened and a servant announced "Monsieur Fortgibu". In walked Fortgibu, who had been invited to another apartment in the same building, and had mistaken the door.

This seems to be a good example of Kammerer's seriality; if there is any "meaning" in the coincidence, it is not apparent. But another example given by Flammarion is a different matter. When he was writing a book a gust of wind carried the pages out of the window; at the same moment it began to rain. He decided there would be no point in going to get them. A few days later the chapter arrived from his printer. It seemed the porter of the printing office had walked past, seen the pages on the ground, and assumed he had dropped them himself; so he gathered them together, sorted them, and delivered them to the printer. What was the subject of the chapter? The wind . . .

So it would seem there are two types of coincidence: serial "clusterings", which are purely "mechanical", and synchronicities, which might seem to imply that the mind itself has been able to influence the laws of nature – as when Rebecca West snatched the book at random off the shelf.

Koestler gives an even stranger example of synchronicity. The writer Pearl Binder was planning a satirical novel in association with two collaborators. They invented a situation in which camps for the homeless had been set up in Hyde Park. They decided to have a refugee Viennese professor, a broken-down old man with a Hungarian-sounding name – such as Horvath-Nadoly. Two days later they read in the newspaper that a homeless foreign old man had been found wandering alone at night in Hyde Park, and had given his name as Horvath-Nadoly. Here all three collaborators had contributed to the impossible coincidence. So if it is to be regarded as "meaningful" rather than an example of "serial clustering", then it has to be supposed that all three participated in some odd form of telepathy and/or precognition; i.e. that called upon to "invent" a situation at random, their unconscious minds preferred to cheat by supplying them with details about a real person – just as, asked to invent a name on the spur of the moment, we shall probably choose a name we have just seen or heard . . .

This "unconscious" explanation – preferred by Jung – can explain dozens of curious coincidences involving literature. In 1898 a novelist named Morgan Robertson wrote a book about a ship called the *Titan*, "the safest vessel in the world", which hit an iceberg on her maiden voyage across the Atlantic; fourteen years later his story came to life in the tragic maiden voyage of the *Titanic*. Moreover, the editor W. T. Stead had written a story about a ship that sank, and concluded: "This is exactly what might take place, and what will take place, if liners are sent to sea short of boats." Like the liner in Morgan Robertson's novel the *Titanic* did *not* have enough boats. And W. T. Stead was one of those who drowned.

In 1855 a playwright named Arthur Law wrote a play about a man called Robert Golding, the sole survivor of the shipwreck of a vessel called the *Caroline*. A few days after it was staged, Law read an account of the sinking of a ship called the *Caroline*; the sole survivor was called Robert Golding.

In 1972 a writer named James Rusk published a pornographic novel called *Black Abductor* under a pseudonym; its plot was so similar to the true story of the kidnapping of heiress Patty Hearst in 1974 by the "Symbionese Liberation Army" – even to the name of the victim, Patricia – that the

FBI later interrogated Rusk to find out if he had been involved in the kidnapping plot. He had not; it was again "pure coincidence".

In the month preceding the Allied invasion of Normandy – D-Day – the *Daily Telegraph* crossword puzzle gave most of the codewords for the operation: Utah, Mulberry, Neptune and Overlord (the last being the name of the whole operation). MI5 was called to investigate, but found that the compiler of the crosswords was a schoolmaster named Dawe who had no idea of how the words had come into his head.

To explain "synchronistic" events, Jung was inclined to refer to a phrase of the French psychologist Pierre Janet, *abaissement du niveau mental*, "lowering of the mental threshold", by which Janet meant a certain lowering of the vital forces – such as we experience when we are tired or discouraged and which is the precondition for neurosis. Jung believed that when the mental threshold is lowered "the tone of the unconscious is heightened, thereby creating a gradient for the unconscious to flow towards the conscious". The conscious then comes under the influence of what Jung calls the "archetypes" or "primordial images". These images belong to the "collective unconscious", and might be – for example – of a "great mother", a hero-god, a devil-figure, or an image of incarnate wisdom. Jung thought that when the archetype is activated, odd coincidences are likely to happen.

Jung worked out his idea of synchronicity with the aid of the physicist Wolfgang Pauli. Pauli himself seemed to have some odd power of causing coincidences. Whenever he touched some piece of experimental apparatus it tended to break. One day in Göttingen a complicated apparatus for studying atomic events collapsed without warning, and Professor J. Franck is said to have remarked: "Pauli must be around somewhere." He wrote to Pauli, and received a reply saying that at the time of the accident his train had been standing in the station at Göttingen, on its way to Copenhagen. Pauli, understandably, was intrigued by Jung's ideas about synchronicity, and Jung's book on the subject was published together with a paper by Pauli, on archetypal ideas in the work of Kepler – Kepler had apparently stumbled on the idea of archetypes three centuries earlier, although he meant something closer to Plato's "ideas". Pauli had created a hypothesis called "the exclusion principle", which says that only one electron at a time can occupy any "planetary orbit" inside an atom. He gave no physical reason for this notion; it simply seemed to him to have a pleasing mathematical symmetry, rather like Avogadro's hypothesis that equal volumes of gases will have equal numbers of molecules. In his own essay on Kepler in *The Encyclopaedia of Philosophy*, Koestler tried to show that Kepler had arrived at his correct results about the solar system through completely nonsensical ideas about the Blessed Trinity and other such notions, the implication being that creative minds have some instinct or intuition that *shows* them scientific truths, on some principle of symmetry or beauty, rather than through logical reasoning. And this in itself implies that there is some strange basic affinity between mind and nature, and that mind is not some accidental product that has no "right" to be in the universe. It was this intuition that drew Jung and Pauli together.

More to the point is a passage in the writing of the medieval "magician" Albertus Magnus:

A certain power to alter things indwells in the human soul and subordinates the other things to her, particularly when she is swept into a great excess of love or hate or the like. When therefore the soul of man falls into a great excess of any passion, it can be proved by experiment that the [excess] binds things together [magically] and alters them in the way it wants. Whoever would learn the secret of doing and undoing these things must know that everyone can influence everything magically if he falls into a great excess.

Strange Tales and Weird Mysteries

That is to say, a psychological state can somehow affect the physical world. But Albertus's "great excess" is clearly the opposite of Jung's "lowering of the mental threshold". One is a lowering of vitality, the other an intensification of it.

Some of the concepts of "split-brain physiology" – a science developed after Jung's death in 1961 – may be able to throw a useful light on these problems. The brain is divided into two hemispheres, rather like a walnut. Brain physiology has established that the left cerebral hemisphere is concerned with our conscious objectives – language, logic, calculation – while the right deals with intuition, pattern-recognition and insight. The remarkable discovery made by Roger Sperry was that when the bridge of nerves – called the *corpus callosum* – which connects the two halves is severed to prevent epilepsy, the patient turns into two people. One split-brain patient tried to hit his wife with one hand while the other held it back. The person I call "me" lives in the left hemisphere; the person who lives in the other half – the "intuitive self" – is a stranger. When a female patient was shown an indecent picture with her right brain, she blushed; asked why she was blushing, she replied: "I don't know."

The right-brain "stranger" is an artist; the left-brain "me" is a scientist. There is some interesting evidence that it is this right-brain "stranger" who is involved in so-called "extra-sensory perception" – telepathy, dowsing, "second sight" – and that his main problem is somehow to communicate the things he knows to the logical self, which is too preoccupied in its own practical purposes to pay attention to the "still, small voice" of the "other self".

The "stranger" can at times "take over". When the English boxer Freddie Mills fought Gus Lesnevitch in 1946, he was knocked down in the second round and concussed. He remembered nothing more until he heard the referee announcing the tenth round. But in the intervening seven rounds he had boxed brilliantly against the much heavier Lesnevitch, and was ahead on points. As soon as he "recovered" consciousness he began to lose. His "other self" had taken over when he was knocked down in the second round. Here is an example where a "lowering of the mental threshold" produced positive results.

If, then, we credit the "other person" with some kind of "extra-sensory perception", it would be possible to explain such phenomena as the activities of "the library angel" – for example, how Rebecca West located the trial she was looking for by reaching out casually. It knows where the trial is located; but it cannot communicate its knowledge to the left brain, which is obsessively searching through the catalogues. Then a librarian approaches, and it sees its chance as he stops near the book. She is prompted to go and complain to the librarian – a relatively easy task, since she is seething with exasperation – and then the "other self" reaches out for the book and, with that intuitive skill that we see in great sportsmen, opens it at the right place . . . (It would be interesting to know if Rebecca West reached out with her left hand – for the left side of the body is controlled by the right brain, and vice versa.)

And how does the ESP hypothesis apply to another story told by Rebecca West and quoted by Koestler? Again she was in the London Library, and had asked an assistant for Gounod's Memoirs. As she was waiting she was approached by an American who had recognized her, and who wanted to know if it was true that she possessed some lithographs by the artist Delpeche. She said she did, and they were still talking when the assistant returned with the book. She opened it casually, and found herself looking at a passage in which Gounod describes how kind Delpeche had been to his mother.

Now here, we can see, the chain of coincidences had been set in motion – by her request for the book – before the stranger came and asked her about Delpeche; so we cannot accuse her "other self" of engineering the whole situation. What we *can* suppose is that the "other self" was somehow aware that the Gounod Memoirs contained a reference to the artist they were speaking about at that very moment, and drew her attention to it by causing her to open the book in the right place . . .

Why? One possible answer is self-evident. Modern man has become a "split-brainer"; for the most part, he lives in the left brain. This means that he is only aware of *half* his identity. Whenever he is reminded of that other half – for example, when music or poetry produce a sudden "warm glow", or when some smell reminds him vividly of child-hood – he experiences the strange sense of wild elation that G. K. Chesterton called "absurd good news". The more he feels "trapped" in his left-brain self by fatigue, discourage-ment, foreboding – the more he actually cuts himself off from that deep inner sense of purpose and well-being. If he had some instant method of re-establishing contact with this inner power – Abraham Maslow called such contacts "peak experiences" – his life would be transformed. It must be irritating for that "other self" to see the left-brain self plunging itself into states of gloom and boredom that are completely unnecessary, and so wasting its life – *both* their lives. So, as a fruitful hypothesis, we might regard "synchronicities" – like the one involving Gounod's Memoirs – as attempts by the "other self" to remind the left-brain personality of its existence, and to rescue it from its sense of "contingency" – the feeling that Proust describes, of feeling "mediocre, accidental, mortal".

There is, unfortunately, another type of synchronicity that cannot be explained on the ESP hypothesis and this is the very type that Jung originally set out to explain. ESP cannot explain how the *I Ching* could produce a "meaningful" answer to a question (if, of course, it actually does so). Common sense tells us that the throwing down of coins can only produce a chance result, *unless* the coins are somehow "interfered with" as they fall. The Chinese believe that the *I Ching* is some kind of living entity – presumably a supernatural one – and we may assume that this entity answers the question by causing the coins to fall in a certain way. The Western psychologist, rejecting the supernatural explanation, can only fall back on the notion that the unconscious mind – the "other self" – can somehow influence the fall of the coins by some form of psychokinesis, "mind over matter". And while this may be more or less satisfactory in explaining how the *I Ching* works, it still fails to explain, for example, the fish synchronicities that Jung found so intriguing: the Latin inscription about a fish, the mention of "April fish", the patient who had painted fish, the embroidery with fish-like monsters, the other patient with the dream of a fish. Psychokinesis can hardly explain this series of coincidences.

This is true also of a type of "cluster" coincidence described by Koestler. A doctor wrote to him commenting that if a patient with some rare and unusual complaint turns up at a surgery, he could be fairly certain that a similar case would turn up later during the same surgery, and that if a patient with a certain name – say, Donnell – should ring him, then another patient called Donnell would be almost certain to turn up at the surgery. Another letter mentioned similar "clusters" of various types: a dentist noting how often he had "runs" of patients with the same kind of extraction problem, an eye specialist noting how often he had runs of patients with the same eye problem, even a typewriter-repairer noticing how often he had runs of the same make of machine for repair, or runs of different machines with the identical problem.

Obviously there can be no "explanation" for such oddities unless a mathematician discovers some completely new law of seriality. But again, we can note that such coincidences tend to produce in us much the same effect as more personal experiences of "serendipity" – a sense that perhaps the universe *is* less meaningless and inscrutable than we assume. And this – as every reader of Jung's book will agree is what

Jung felt about synchronicity. In fact, a hostile critic might object that Jung – who was the son of a parson – is trying to introduce God by the back door. All his attempts to argue in favour of a "scientific" principle of synchronicity are unconvincing because the words "acausal connecting principle" involve a contradiction in terms – unless, that is, he is willing to admit that it is "pure chance", in which case he has undermined his own argument. A coincidence is either "meaningful" or it is not; and if it is meaningful, then it is not a coincidence.

In the last analysis, accepting or rejecting "synchronicity" is a matter of individual temperament. I personally am inclined to accept it because my own experience of "coincidences" inclines me to the belief that they *are* often "meaningful". On the morning when I was about to begin the article on Joan of Arc *(see* page 37), I noticed in my library a bound series of the *International History Magazine,* and decided to spend half an hour looking through it in case it contained material for this book. I opened the first volume at random, and found myself looking at an article on Joan of Arc, whose editorial introduction raised the question of whether she survived her "execution". In fact, the article proved to be useless: the author made no mention of the controversy about the Dame des Armoires. Does this not in itself suggest that the coincidence was "non-meaningful"? Not necessarily. I have cited elsewhere Jacques Vallée's interesting theory about synchronicity. When he was researching a cult that used the name of the prophet Melchizedek, he spent a great deal of time looking up every reference to Melchizedek he could find. In Los Angeles he asked a woman taxi driver for a receipt: it was signed M. Melchizedek. A check with the Los Angeles telephone directory revealed that there was only one Melchizedek in the whole area.

Vallée points out that there are two ways in which a librarian can store information. One is to place it in alphabetical order on shelves. But computer scientists have discovered that there is a simpler and quicker method. They prefer to store information as it arrives – the equivalent of a librarian putting books on the shelves side by side as they come into the – library and having a keyword or algorithm that will retrieve it. (In a library, the equivalent might be as follows: as each new book comes into the library, some kind of "beeping" mechanism is attached to its spine; each beeper is adjusted to respond to a certain number code, like a telephone. When the librarian requires a certain book, he dials the number on his pocket beeper, and then goes straight to the book that is beeping.)

Vallée suggests that "the world might be organized more like a randomized data base than a sequential library". It was as if he had stuck on the universal notice-board a note saying; "Wanted, Melchizedeks", and some earnest librarian had said: "How about this one?" "No, that's no good – that's just a taxi driver . . ."

This picture, like Jung's, suggests that there *is* some mutual interaction between the mind and the universe, and that the key to "retrieving information" is to be in the right state of mind: a state of deep interest or excitement: Albertus Magnus's "excess of passion".

Another personal example. I was led to write the present article partly by the "Joan of Arc coincidence", partly by another coincidence that happened a day or two later. I had received in the post a copy of the biography of the American novelist Ayn Rand by Barbara Branden. I was reading this in bed the next day when the post arrived. This included a paperback novel sent to me by an American reader, with a letter enclosed. The letter began: "In Barbara Branden's recent biography of Ayn Rand you are mentioned in a footnote . . ."

Half an hour later, about to go to my study, I noticed a newspaper clipping that my wife had left for me outside the door. I asked her "What's this?" and she said: "It's an article

that mentions Hemingway – I thought it might interest you."
In fact it was the article about coincidence and lost manuscripts by Godfrey Smith, quoted at the beginning of the
present article.

As it happened, I decided not to write the coincidence
article immediately; I had planned first of all to write a piece
about the disappearance of Mary Rogers. I took Poe's short
stories from my bookshelf and opened it at "The Mystery of
Marie Roget". The opening paragraph reads: "There are few
persons, even among the calmest thinkers, who have not
occasionally been startled into a vague yet thrilling half-
credence in the supernatural, by *coincidences* of so seemingly
marvellous a character that, as mere coincidences, the
intellect has been unable to receive them." It confirmed my
decision to write this article.

As if to underline this point, a further coincidence
occurred after I had written the preceding sentence, which
happened to be at the end of a day's work. About to leave my
study, I noticed among an untidy pile of books a title I had
no recollection of seeing before: *You Are Sentenced to Life* by
W. D. Chesney, published by a private press in California; it
was a book about life after death. I had obviously bought it a
long time ago and had never – as far as I know – even
glanced into it. I decided it was time to remedy this. Later in
the afternoon, I spent an hour glancing through it, reading a
section here and there; then, just before closing it, I decided
to glance at the very end. The top of the last page was
headed: ORDER OF MELCHIZEDEK, and was a reprint of a
letter from Grace Hooper Pettipher, "Instructor within the
Order of Melchizedek", requesting a copy of another book
published by the same press. I doubt whether, in two
thousand or so books in my study, there is another reference
to Melchizedek; but I had to stumble upon this one after
writing about Melchizedek in an article about synchronicity.

It is my own experience that coincidences like this seem to
happen when I am in "good form" – when I am feeling alert,

cheerful and optimistic, and not when I am feeling tired, bored or gloomy. This leads me to formulate my own hypothesis about synchronicity as follows. As a writer, I am at my best when I feel alert and purposeful; at these times I feel a sense of "hidden meanings" lurking behind the apparently impassive face of everyday reality. But this is not true only for writers; it applies to all human beings. We are *all* at our best when the imagination is awake, and we can sense the presence of that "other self", the intuitive part of us. When we are tired or discouraged we feel "stranded" in left-brain consciousness. We feel, as William James says, that "our fires are damped, our draughts are checked". We can be jarred out of this state by a sudden crisis, or any pleasant stimulus, but more often than not these fail to present themselves. It must be irritating for "the other self" to find its partner so dull and sluggish, allowing valuable time and opportunity to leak away by default. A "synchronicity" can snap us into a sudden state of alertness and awareness. And if the "other self" can, by the use of its peculiar powers, bring about a synchronicity, then there is still time to prevent us from wasting yet another day of our brief lives.

The Melchizedek coincidence seems to me of another kind, designed to confirm that we are on "the right track". When in the late 1960s I first turned my attention to the field of the paranormal, and began writing a book called *The Occult*, such coincidences became commonplace. I have described in that book how I needed a reference from some alchemical text. I knew that the book containing the reference was in one of the books facing my desk; but it was towards the end of the day, and I was feeling tired and lazy. Besides, I had forgotten where to find the reference, and my heart sank at the prospect of a fruitless search through half a dozen volumes . . . Conscience finally triumphed and I heaved myself to my feet, crossed the room, and took a book off the shelf. As I did so the next book fell off the shelf; it landed on the floor, open, at the passage I was looking for. And I felt that curious flash of gratitude and delight that we always experience in these moments, as if some invisible guardian angel has politely tendered his help.

Now, a book falling off a shelf and opening at the right page is obviously closer to the procedure of the *I Ching* than, for example, Mrs Kammerer's chain of coincidences about Prince Rohan and Lake Attersee, or Flammarion's story about M. Fortgibu. Yet it seems equally obvious that, in a basic sense, there is a family resemblance between them. The problem arises if we attempt some kind of classification. When Rebecca West reached out and found the right book, this sounds like ESP. But a book falling off a shelf at the right page obviously involves some extra element besides ESP – something closer to psychokinesis. But neither ESP nor psychokinesis can begin to explain Mrs Kammerer's chain of coincidences; and in the case of M. Fortgibu and the plum pudding, it becomes absurd. We seem to be dealing with the mysterious entity that Charles Fort called "the cosmic joker", and any respectable parapsychologist is bound to draw back in horror at the very idea.

But even if synchronicity declines to fit into any of our scientific theories, this is no reason to refuse to believe in its existence. Science still has no idea of how or why the universe began, of the nature of time, or of what lies beyond the outermost limit of the stars. In fact, science continues to use terms like space, time and motion *as if* they were comprehensible to the human intellect; no one accuses Cantor of being an occultist or mystic because he devised a mathematics of infinity. Science continues to grow and develop in spite of its uneasy metaphysical foundations.

From the purely practical point of view, the chief problem of human existence is individual lack of purpose. In those curious moments of relaxation or sudden happiness that we all experience at intervals, we can see that it is stupid to lose purpose and direction, and that if only we could learn to summon this insight *at will*, this fatal tendency to forgetfulness could be permanently eradicated, and life would be transformed. It is obvious in such moments that if we could train ourselves to behave *as if* there were hidden meanings lurking behind the blank face of the present, the problem would be solved. If "synchronicities" can produce that sense of meaning and purpose, then it is obviously sensible for us to behave as if they were meaningful coincidences, and to ignore the question of their scientific validity.

Chapter Fifteen

Spontaneous Human Combustion

On the evening of Sunday, 1 July 1951 Mrs Mary Reeser, aged seventy-seven, seemed slightly depressed as she sat in her overstuffed armchair and smoked a cigarette. At about 9 p.m. her landlady, Mrs Pansy Carpenter, called in to say goodnight. Mrs Reeser showed no disposition to go to bed yet; it was a hot evening in St Petersburg, Florida.

At five the next morning, Mrs Carpenter awoke to a smell of smoke; assuming it was a water pump that had been overheating, she went to the garage and turned it off. She was awakened again at eight by a telegraph boy with a telegram for Mrs Reeser; Mrs Carpenter signed for it and took it up to Mrs Reeser's room. To her surprise, the doorknob was hot. She shouted for help, and two decorators working across the street came in. One of them placed a cloth over the doorknob and turned it; a blast of hot air met him as the door opened. Yet the place seemed empty, and at first they could see no sign of fire. Then they noticed a blackened circle on the carpet where the armchair had stood. Only a few springs now remained. In the midst of them there was a human skull "charred to the size of a baseball", and a fragment of liver attached to a backbone. There was also a foot encased in a satin slipper; it had been burnt down to the ankle.

Mrs Reeser was a victim of a baffling phenomenon called spontaneous human combustion; there are hundreds of recorded cases. Yet in their standard textbook *Forensic Medicine*, Drs S. A. Smith and F. S. Fiddes assert flatly:

Drawing by Phiz for Dickens's *Bleak House* showing an act of spontaneous human combustion.

"Spontaneous combustion of the human body cannot occur, and no good purpose can be served by discussing it." This is a typical example of the kind of wishful thinking in which scientists are prone to indulge when they confront a fact that falls outside the range of their experience. In the same way the great chemist Lavoisier denied the possibility of meteorites.

The example of Mrs Reeser is worth citing because it is mentioned by Professor John Taylor in his book *Science and the Supenatural*, a book whose chief purpose is to debunk the whole idea of the "paranormal", which, according to Professor Taylor, tends to "crumble to nothing" as it is scientifically appraised. Yet he then proceeds to admit that there are instances that seem "reasonably well validated", and proceeds to cite the case of Mrs Reeser.

Twenty-nine years later, in October 1980, a case of spontaneous combustion was observed at close quarters when a naval airwoman named Jeanna Winchester was driving with a friend, Leslie Scott, along Seaboard Avenue in Jacksonville, Florida. Suddenly, Jeanna Winchester burst into yellow flames, and screamed, "Get me out of here." Her companion tried to beat out the flames with her hands, and the car ran into a telegraph pole. When Jeanna Winchester was examined it was found that twenty per cent of her body was covered with burns. But Jeanna Winchester survived.

Michael Harrison's book on spontaneous combustion, *Fire From Heaven* (1976), cites dozens of cases; they make it clear that the chief mystery of spontaneous combustion is that it seldom spreads beyond the person concerned. On Whit Monday 1725, in Rheims, Nicole Millet, the wife of the landlord of the Lion d'Or, was found burnt to death in an *unburnt* armchair, and her husband was accused of her murder. But a young surgeon, Claude-Nicholas Le Cat, succeeded in persuading the court that spontaneous human combustion *does* occur, and Millet was acquitted – the verdict was that his wife had died "by a visitation of God". The case inspired a Frenchman called Jonas Dupont to gather together all the evidence he could find for spontaneous combustion, which he published in a book *De Incendiis Corporis Humani Spontaneis*, printed in Leyden in 1763.

Another famous case of this period was that of Countess Cornelia di Bandi, of Cesena, aged sixty-two, who was found on the floor of her bedroom by her maid. Her stockinged legs were untouched, and between them lay her head, half burnt. The rest of the body was reduced to ashes, and the air was full of floating soot. The bed was undamaged and the sheets had been thrown back, as if she had got out – perhaps to open a window – and then been quickly consumed as she stood upright, so the head had fallen between the legs. Unlike the wife of innkeeper Millet, the countess had not been a heavy drinker. (One of the most popular theories of spontaneous combustion at this period was that it was due to large quantities of alcohol in the body.)

Two nineteenth-century novelists used spontaneous combustion to dispose of unwanted characters. Captain Marryat borrowed details from a *Times* report of 1832 to describe the death of the mother of his hero Jacob Faithful (in the novel of the same name), who is reduced to "a sort of unctuous pitchy cinder" in her bed. Twenty years later, in 1852, Dickens put an end to his drunken rag-and-bone dealer Krook in *Bleak House* by means of spontaneous combustion – Krook is charred to a cinder that looks like a burnt log. G. H. Lewes, George Eliot's lover, took issue with Dickens and declared that spontaneous combustion was impossible, so in his preface to *Bleak House* Dickens contradicts Lewes and cites thirty examples from press reports. Yet at the end of his article on Krook in *The Dickens Encyclopaedia* (1924), Arthur L. Hayward states dogmatically: "The possibility of spontaneous combustion in human beings has been finally disproved." He fails to explain what experiments have "finally disproved" it.

Harrison's book, which gathers together the result of many studies, leaves no possible doubt of the reality of spontaneous combustion. But what causes it? At present it must be confessed that the phenomenon baffles medical knowledge. But Harrison offers some interesting clues. He speaks of the researches of an American doctor, Mayne R. Coe Junior, who was interested in the subject of telekinesis – mind over matter. Coe was able to move aluminium strips pivoted on the points of needles by moving his hand over them – this was obviously due to some natural physical "magnetism". He began various yoga exercises in an attempt to develop his bioelectricity; sitting one day in an easy-chair, he felt a powerful current passing downwards from his head throughout his body; he thought it was of high voltage but low amperage. He suspended a cardboard box from the ceiling on a length of string, and found that he could cause it to move from a distance – when the room was dry, from as much as eight feet. He then charged his body with 35,000 volts DC, using an electric current, and found that he could move the box in exactly the same way. This seemed to prove that he was in fact generating a high voltage current with his mental exercises. He also went up in an aeroplane to an altitude of 21,000 feet, where the air was extremely dry, and produced electric sparks after he had charged his body to 35,000 volts. Coe theorized that this could explain the phenomenon of levitation when the yogi's body floats off the ground – with the positively charged human body repelling the negatively charged earth.

Harrison also cites cases of human "batteries" and magnets, people (usually children) who have developed a powerful electric charge. In 1877 Caroline Clare of London, Ontario, turned into a human magnet, who attracted metal objects and could give a powerful electric shock to as many as twenty people holding hands. She was suffering from adolescent depressions at the time. Frank McKinistry of Joplin, Missouri, developed a magnetic force which caused his feet to stick to the earth. In 1895 fourteen-year-old Jennie Morgan of Sedalia, Missouri, generated a charge sufficient to knock a grown man on his back, and when she touched a pump handle sparks flew from her fingertips. It is also worth noting that many teenagers who became the focus of "poltergeist effects" developed magnetic or electrical properties; in 1846 a French girl named Angélique Cottin became a kind of human electric battery; objects that touched her flew off violently, and a heavy oak loom began to dance when she came near it. On the other hand, Esther Cox, the "focus" of the disturbances at Great Amherst in Nova Scotia, developed a magnetism that made cutlery fly to her and stick fast. It seems that there must be two kinds of charges, positive and negative.

Spontaneous Human Combustion

According to Dr Coe, each human muscle cell is a battery, and a cubic inch could develop 400,000 volts. (The inventor Nicola Tesla used to demonstrate that the human body can take immense electrical charges – enough to light up neon tubes – provided the amperage is kept very low.)

But this seems unlikely to explain spontaneous combustion: the whole point of Tesla's experiments was that he did *not* burst into flame. It is high amperage that can cause "burn-ups". (If two 12-volt car batteries are connected by thin wire, the wire will melt; even thick wire becomes hot.) And this could begin to explain why the surroundings of the victim of spontaneous combustion are undamaged; they are non-conductors.

Victims of spontaneous combustion tend to be the old and the young. On 27 August 1938, the twenty-two-year-old Phyllis Newcombe was dancing vigorously in Chelmsford, Essex, when her body glowed with a blue light which turned into flames; she died within minutes. In October of the same year a girl called Maybelle Andrews was dancing in a Soho nightclub with her boyfriend, Billy Clifford, when flames erupted from her back, chest and shoulders. Her boyfriend, who was badly burned trying to put her out, said that there were no flames in the room – the flames seemed to come from the girl herself. She died on the way to hospital. In such cases it seems just conceivable that the activity of dancing built up some kind of static electricity. Michael Harrison even points out that "ritual dancing" is used by primitive tribes to build up emotional tension in religious ceremonies, and suggests that this is what has happened here.

Michael Harrison also points out some curious geographical links. On 13 March 1966 three men were "spontaneously combusted" at the same time. John Greeley, helmsman of the SS *Ulrich*, was burnt to a cinder some miles west of Land's End; George Turner a lorry-driver, was found burnt at the wheel of his lorry at Upton-by-Chester – the lorry overturned in a ditch; in Nijmegen, Holland, eighteen-year-old Willem ten Bruik died at the wheel of his car. As usual in such cases, the surroundings of all three were undamaged. Harrison points out that the three men were at the points of an equilateral triangle whose sides were 340 miles long. Is it conceivable that the earth itself discharged energy in a triangular pattern?

Another investigator, Larry Arnold, put forward his own theory in the magazine *Frontiers of Science* (January 1982): that so-called "ley lines" – lines of "earth force" – may be involved. The man who "discovered" ley lines, Alfred Watkins, noted how frequently places called "Brent" occur on them (brent being an old English form of "burnt"). Other "ley-hunters" have suggested that megalithic stone circles are placed at crucial points on ley lines – often at crossing-points of several leys. It is again interesting to note how many stone circles are associated with the idea of dancing – for example, the Merry Maidens in Cornwall; Stonehenge itself was known as "the Giants' Dance". It has been suggested that ritual dances occurred at these sites, so that the dancers would somehow interact with the earth energy (or "telluric force").

Larry Arnold drew a dozen or so major leys on a map of England, then set out to find if they were associated with mystery fires. He claims that one 400-mile-long "fire-leyne" (as he calls them) passed through five towns where ten mysterious blazes had occurred. He also notes several cases of spontaneous combustion occurring on this "leyne". He cites four cases which occurred on it between 1852 and 1908.

Harrison believes that spontaneous combustion is basically a "mental freak", where the mind somehow influences the body to build up immense charges. The answer could lie in either of the two theories, or in a combination of the two.

Chapter Sixteen

The Great
Tunguska Explosion

On 30 June 1908 the inhabitants of Nizhne-Karelinsk, a small village in central Siberia, saw a bluish-white streak of fire cut vertically across the sky to the northwest. What began as a bright point of light lengthened over a period of ten minutes until it seemed to split the sky in two. When it reached the ground it shattered to form a monstrous cloud of black smoke. Seconds later there was a terrific roaring detonation that made the buildings tremble. Assuming that the Day of Judgement had arrived, many of the villagers fell on their knees. The reaction was not entirely absurd; in fact, they had witnessed the greatest natural disaster in the earth's recorded history. If the object that caused what is now known as "the Great Siberian Explosion" had arrived a few hours earlier or later it might have landed in more heavily populated regions, and caused millions of deaths.

As it later turned out, the village of Nizhne-Karelinsk had been over 200 miles away from the "impact point", and yet the explosion had been enough to shake debris from their roofs. A Trans-Siberian express train stopped because the driver was convinced that it was derailed, and seismographs in the town of Irkutsk indicated a crash of earthquake proportions. Both the train and the town were over 800 miles from the explosion.

Whatever it was that struck the Tunguska region of the Siberian forestland had exploded with a force never before imagined. Its shockwave travelled around the globe twice before it died out, and its general effect on the weather in the

127

northern hemisphere was far-reaching. During the rest of June it was quite possible to read the small print in the London *Times* at midnight. There were photographs of Stockholm taken at 1 o'clock in the morning by natural light, and a photograph of the Russian town of Navrochat taken at midnight looks like a bright summer afternoon.

For some months the world was treated to spectacular dawns and sunsets, as impressive as those that had been seen after the great Krakatoa eruption in 1883. From this, as well as the various reports of unusual cloud formations over following months, it is fair to guess that the event had thrown a good deal of dust into the atmosphere, as happens with violent volcanic eruptions and, notably, atomic explosions.

Perhaps the strangest aspect of the Great Siberian Explosion was that no one paid much attention to it. Reports of the falling object were published in Siberian newspapers but did not spread any further. Meteorologists speculated about the strange weather, but no one came close to guessing its real cause.

It was not until the Great War had been fought, and the Russian Revolution had overthrown the tsarist regime that the extraordinary events of that June day finally reached the general public. In 1921, as part of Lenin's general plan to place the USSR at the forefront of world science, the Soviet Academy of Sciences commissioned Leonid Kulik to investigate meteorite falls on Soviet territory. It was Kulik who stumbled upon the few brief reports in ten-year-old Siberian newspapers that finally led him to suspect that something extraordinary had happened in central Siberia in the summer of 1908.

Leonid found the reports confusing and contradictory. None of them seemed to agree quite where the object had exploded. Some even claimed that the "meteor" had later been found. But when his researchers began to collect eyewitness reports of the event Kulik became convinced that whatever had exploded in the Tunguska forest was certainly not a normal meteorite.

These reports described how the ground had opened up to release a great pillar of fire and smoke which burned brighter than the sun. Distant huts were blown down and reindeer herds scattered. A man ploughing in an open field felt his shirt burning on his back, and others described being badly sunburnt on one side of the face but not the other. Many people claimed to have been made temporarily deaf by the noise, or to have suffered long-term effects of shock. Yet, almost unbelievably, not a single person had been killed or seriously injured. Whatever it was that produced the explosion had landed in one of the few places on earth where its catastrophic effect was minimized. A few hours later, and it could have obliterated St Petersburg, London or New York. Even if it had landed in the sea, tidal waves might have destroyed whole coastal regions. That day the human race had escaped the greatest disaster in its history, and had not even been aware of it.

Finally Kulik discovered that a local meteorologist had made an estimate of the point of impact, and in 1927 he was given the necessary backing by the Academy of Sciences to find the point where the "great meteorite" had fallen.

The great Siberian forest is one of the least accessible places on earth. Even today it remains largely unexplored, and there are whole areas that have only ever been surveyed from the air. What settlements there are can be found along the banks of its mighty rivers, some of them miles in width. The winters are ferociously cold, and in the summer the ground becomes boggy, and the air is filled with the hum of mosquitoes. Kulik was faced with an almost impossible task: to travel by horse and raft with no idea of exactly where to look or what to look for.

In March 1927 he set off accompanied by two local guides who had witnessed the event, and after many setbacks arrived on the banks of the Mekirta river in April. The

Mekirta is the closest river to the impact point, and in 1927 formed a boundary between untouched forest and almost total devastation.

On that first day Kulik stood on a low hill and surveyed the destruction caused by the Tunguska explosion. For as far as he could see to the north – perhaps a dozen miles – there was not one full-gown tree left standing. Every one had been flattened by the blast, and they lay like a slaughtered regiment, all pointing towards him. Yet it was obvious that what he was looking at was only a fraction of the devastation, since all the trees were facing in the same direction as far as the horizon. The blast must have been far greater than even the wildest reports had suggested.

Kulik wanted to explore the devastation; his two guides were terrified, and refused to go on. So Kulik was forced to return with them, and it was not until June that he managed to return with two new companions.

The expedition followed the line of broken trees for several days until they came to a natural amphitheatre in the hills, and pitched camp there. They spent the next few days surveying the surrounding area, and Kulik reached the conclusion that "the cauldron" as he called it, was the centre of the blast. All around, the fallen trees faced away from it, and yet, incredibly, some trees actually remained standing although stripped and charred, at the very centre of the explosion.

The full extent of the desolation was now apparent; from the river to its central point was a distance of thirty-seven miles. So the blast had flattened more than four thousand square miles of forest.

Still working on the supposition that the explosion had been caused by a large meteorite, Kulik began searching the area for its remains. He thought he had achieved his object when he discovered a number of pits filled with water – he naturally assumed that they had been made by fragments of the exploding meteorite. Yet when the holes were drained they were found to be empty. One even had a tree-stump at the bottom, proving it had not been made by a blast.

Kulik was to make four expeditions to the area of the explosion, and until his death he remained convinced that it had been caused by an unusually large meteorite. Yet he never found the iron or rock fragments that would provide him with the evidence he needed. In fact, he never succeeded in proving that anything had even struck the ground. There was evidence of two blast waves – the original explosion and the ballistic wave – and even of brief flash fire; but there was no crater.

The new evidence only deepened the riddle. An aerial survey in 1938 showed that only 770 square miles of forest had been flattened, and that at the very point where the crater should have been the original trees were still standing. That suggested the vagaries of an exploding bomb, rather than that of the impact of a giant meteor – like the one that made the 600-foot-deep crater at Winslow, Arizona.

Even the way that the object fell to earth was disputed. Over seven hundred eyewitnesses claimed that it changed course as it fell, saying that it was originally moving towards Lake Baikal before it swerved. Falling heavenly bodies have never been known to do this, nor is it possible to explain how it could have happened in terms of physical dynamics.

Another curious puzzle about the explosion was its effect on the trees and insect life in the blast area. Trees that had survived the explosion had either stopped growing, or were shooting up at a greatly accelerated rate. Later studies revealed new species of ants and other insects which are peculiar to the Tunguska blast region.

It was not until some years after Kulik's death in a German prisoner-of-war camp that scientists began to see similarities between the Tunguska event and another even more catastrophic explosion: the destruction of Hiroshima and Nagasaki with thermonuclear devices.

Our knowledge of the atom bomb enables us to clear up

many of the mysteries that baffled Kulik. The reason there was no crater was that the explosion confirmed this; at both Nagasaki and Hiroshima, buildings directly beneath the blast remained standing, because the blast spread sideways. Genetic mutations in the flora and fauna around the Japanese cities are like those witnessed in Siberia, while blisters found on dogs and reindeer in the Tunguska area can now be recognized as radiation burns.

Atomic explosions produce disturbances in the earth's magnetic field, and even today the area around the Tunguska explosion has been described as "magnetic chaos". It seems clear that an electro-magnetic "hurricane" of incredible strength has ruptured the earth's magnetic field in this area.

Eyewitness accounts of the cloud produced by the explosion again support the view that it was some kind of atomic device; it had the typical shape of the atomic "mushroom cloud". Unfortunately, the one conclusive piece of evidence for the "atom bomb" theory is lacking: by the time the area's radiation levels were tested, more than fifty years later, they were normal.

Later investigators also learned that Kulik had been mistaken in his theory about the water-filled holes; they were not caused by meteorite fragments but by winter ice forcing its way to the surface through expansion, then melting in summer. Kulik's immense labours to drain the holes had been a waste of time.

Unfortunately, none of the new evidence that has been uncovered by Russian – and even American – expeditions has thrown any light on the cause of the explosion. UFO enthusiasts favour the theory that the object was an alien space craft, powered by atomic motors, which went out of control as it struck the earth's atmosphere. It has even been suggested that such a space craft might have headed towards Lake Baikal because it was in need of fresh water to cool its nuclear reactors; before it could reach its objective the reactors superheated and exploded.

The Great Tunguska Explosion

The scientific establishment is naturally inclined to discount this theory as pure fantasy. But some of its own hypotheses seem equally fantastic. A. A. Jackson and M. P. Ryan of the University of Texas have suggested that the explosion was caused by a miniature black hole – a kind of whirlpool in space caused by the total collapse of the particles inside the atom. They calculated that their black hole would have passed straight through the earth and come out on the other side, and the Russians were sufficiently impressed by the theory to research local newspapers in Iceland and Newfoundland for June 1908; but there was no sign of the Tunguska-like catastrophe that should have occurred if Jackson and Ryan were correct.

Other American scientists suggested that the explosion was caused by anti-matter, a hypothetical type of matter whose particles contain the opposite electric charge to those of normal matter. In contact with normal matter, anti-matter would explode and simply disappear. Only atomic radiation would be left behind. But there is even less evidence to support this theory than there is for the black-hole explanation.

Slightly more plausible – but still highly improbable – is the theory of the English scientist Frank Whipple that the earth had been struck by a comet. Astronomers still have no idea where comets originate, or how they are formed. The two chief objections to the comet theory are that it would be unlikely to produce a "nuclear" explosion, and that it would have been observed by astronomers long before it reached the earth. Supporters of the comet theory have pointed out that a comet coming in from the direction of the sun might be very hard to detect; and that the explosion of a comet might produce an effect similar to that of solar flares, which produce radio-activity. But none of the 120 observatories questioned by the Russians have any record of a comet on the trajectory of the Tunguska object.

More recently, it has been pointed out that the Tunguska

event took place on 30 June and that on that same day each year the earth's orbit crosses that of a meteor stream called Beta Taurids, producing a "meteor shower". If one of these meteors had been exceptionally large, it could have survived burning up in the earth's atmosphere, and as its super-heated exterior reacted against its frozen interior, it would have shattered like molten glass suddenly plunged into freezing water. If this theory is correct, then it seems that Kulik was right after all. But that only reminds us that Kulik was unable to find the slightest shred of evidence for his theory. Eight decades after it took place, it seems increasingly unlikely that the mystery of the Tunguska explosion will ever be solved.

Does the woolly mammoth still wander the Siberian forests? The last examples are generally thought to have died out ten thousand years ago. Their frozen bodies are discovered from time to time, sometimes in almost perfect condition, locked in ice. More often their tusks are uncovered and sold by the Yakuts or other tribes of the north. It has been estimated that up to 100,000 mammoth tusks have been disinterred in the last three hundred years. There is no doubt that the mammoths so recovered died in antiquity. However modern eyewitness accounts of live mammoths continue to surface.

In 1918 an elderly huntsman told the French consul in Vladivostok of the "chestnut-coloured elephants" that he had once tracked. He had come across a huge trampled path running across the forest, and had decided to follow it. After several days he caught sight of one of the animals responsible. His description exactly matched that of a mammoth: larger than a modern elephant (a beast that the huntsman had never seen) and covered in shaggy chestnut hair.

The Soviet Academy of Science treats the sightings of mammoths as genuine evidence, assigning research staff to investigate them. The argument that such beasts could not remain hidden from modern man does not take into account the vast and relatively unexplored areas of Siberia. There are also the many instances of supposedly extinct creatures being found to still exist, merely shying away from man's presence in their territories: the coelacanth, the okapi, the Chacoan pessary . . .

There may yet be many creatures that we have only succeeded in catching in their fossilized form.

Chapter Seventeen

Velikovsky's Comet

When the bulky manuscript of *Worlds in Collision* landed on the desk of a New York editor in 1947 its tattered state left no doubt that it had been rejected many times. All the same, the editor was impressed. According to the author, Immanuel Velikovsky, the earth had been almost destroyed about three and a half thousand years ago by a near-collision with a comet; in the earthquakes and volcanic eruptions that followed, cities were wiped out and whole countries laid waste. It was a fascinating and erudite book, and its author – who was apparently a respectable psychiatrist – had the ability to write a clear and vigorous prose.

The editor cautiously recommended it. His superiors were worried; Macmillan was a reputable publisher with a large textbook list; they could not afford to be accused of encouraging the lunatic fringe. So they compromised, and offered Velikovsky a small advance and a contract that gave them the option to publish, but no guarantee that they would do so. A year later they finally decided to go ahead, and *Worlds in Collision* made its belated appearance on 3 April 1950. Within days it had climbed to the top of the best-seller list. When it appeared in England the following September its reputation had preceded it, so that it sold out its first impression even before publication. But by that time Macmillan's doubts had been justified; the denunciations of the book were so violent that they were forced into retreat, and *Worlds in Collision* had to be passed on to another publisher. By then Velikovsky had become one of the most famous and most vilified men in America.

Who was this controversial psychiatrist who also seemed

to be an expert on astronomy, geology and world history? Immanuel Velikovsky was a Russian Jew, born in Vitebsk in June 1895, who had studied mathematics in Moscow. He went on to study medicine, qualifying in 1921, then studied psychiatry in Vienna with Freud's pupil Stekel. In 1924 he moved to Palestine to practise, and became increasingly interested in Biblical archaeology. The turning-point in his career was a reading of Freud's *Moses and Monotheism* (1937). In this book Freud proposes that Moses was not a Jew but an Egyptian, and that he was a follower of the monotheistic religion of the pharaoh Akhnaton, the king who replaced the host of Egyptian gods with one single sun god. Freud proposed that Moses fled from Egypt after the death of Akhnaton (probably murdered) and imposed his religion on the Jews.

The obvious historical objection to this theory is that Moses is supposed to have lived about a century after the death of Akhnaton; but Freud contested this view, and moved fearlessly into the arena of historical research. Dazzled by his boldness, Velikovsky decided to do the same. His researches into Egyptian, Greek and Near Eastern history soon convinced him that much of the accepted dating is hopelessly wrong. But they led him to an even more unorthodox conclusion: that the pharaoh Akhnaton was none other than the legendary Oedipus of Greek myth, and that the story arose out of the fact that Akhnaton had murdered his father and married his mother.

Velikovsky went on to construct a theory beside which even Freud's heterodox views seemed conservative; that the various events that accompanied the plagues of Egypt – the crossing of the Red Sea, the destruction of the Egyptian armies by floods, the manna that fell from heaven – were the outcome of some great cosmic upheaval. And at this point Velikovsky came across exactly what he was looking for: a papyrus written by an Egyptian sage called Ipuwer, which contained an account of events that sounded strangely like the Bible story in Exodus.

In 1939 Velikovsky moved to the United States, and continued his researches in its libraries. What precisely was the "great catastrophe"? The Austrian Hanns Hoerbiger had put forward the theory that the earth has had several moons, and that the collapse of one of these moons on the earth caused the great floods and upheavals recorded in the Bible and in other ancient documents. But Velikovsky came to reject the Hoerbiger theory. There was a far more exciting clue. Before the second millennium BC – and even later – the planet Venus was not grouped by ancient astronomers with the other planets. That might have been because it was so close to the sun that they mistook it for a star – in fact, it is called the morning star. But what if it was because Venus was not in its present position at that time? Velikovsky found tantalizing references in old documents to something that sounded like a near-collision of a comet with the earth. In legends from Greece to Mexico he found suggestions that this catastrophe was somehow linked with Venus. Only one thing puzzled him deeply: that other legends seemed to link the catastrophe with Zeus, the father of the gods, also known as Jupiter. He finally reconciled these stories by reaching the astonishing conclusion that Venus was "born out of" Jupiter – forced out by a gigantic explosion. Venus began as a comet, and passed so close to Mars that it was dragged out of its orbit; then it came close to earth, causing the Biblical catastrophes; then it finally settled down near the sun as the planet Venus.

It sounds like pure lunacy; but Velikovsky argued it with formidable erudition. And, unlike the usual crank, he spent a great deal of time searching for scientific evidence. He needed, for example, a spectroscopic analysis of the atmospheres of Mars and Venus, and he decided to approach the eminent astronomer Harlow Shapley. Shapley had himself become a figure of controversy in 1919 when he announced his conclusion that our solar system is not – as had previously been believed – at the centre of the Milky Way, but somewhere much closer to its edge; perhaps it was the blow to human self-esteem that caused the opposition. At all events, Velikovsky seems to have reasoned that Shapley might be sympathetic to his own heterodox ideas. Shapley was polite, but said he was too busy to read *Worlds in Collision*; he asked a colleague, a sociologist named Horace Kallen, if he would read it first. Kallen did so, and was excited; he told Shapley that it seemed a serious and worthwhile book, and that even if it should prove to be nonsense, it was still a bold and fascinating thesis. The Macmillan editor agreed, and Velikovsky got his contract.

Three months before its publication, in January 1950, a preview of *Worlds in Collision* appeared in *Harper's* magazine, and aroused widespread interest. Shapley's reaction was curious. He wrote Macmillan a letter saying that he had heard that they had decided *not* to publish the book after all, and that he was greatly relieved; he had discussed it with various scientists, and they were all astonished that Macmillan should venture into "the Black Arts".

Macmillan replied defensively that the book was not supposed to be hard science, but was a controversial theory that scholars ought to know about. Shapley replied tartly that Velikovsky was "complete nonsense", and that when he had introduced himself to Shapley in a New York hotel, Shapley had looked around to see if he had his keeper with him. The book, he said, was "quite possibly intellectually fraudulent", a legpull designed to make money, and if Macmillan insisted on publishing it, then they had better drop Shapley from their list.

Macmillan ignored this attempt at blackmail, and published the book in April. No doubt they were astonished to find that they had a best-seller on their hands. America has a vast audience of "fundamentalists" – people who believe that every word of the Bible is literally true, and are delighted to read anything that seems to offer scientific support for this view. (The same audience made Werner Keller's *The Bible as History* a best-seller in 1956.) Now they rushed to buy this book that seemed to prove that the parting of the Red Sea and the destruction of the walls of Jericho had really taken place. So did thousands of ordinary intelligent readers who simply enjoyed an adventure in speculative thought.

Scientists did not share this open-mindedness. One exception was Gordon Atwater, chairman of the astronomy department at New York's Museum of Natural History; he published a review urging that scientists ought to be willing to consider the book without prejudice; the review resulted in his dismissal. James Putnam, the editor who accepted *Worlds in Collision*, was dismissed from Macmillan. Professors deluged Macmillan with letters threatening to boycott their textbooks unless *Worlds in Collision* was withdrawn. Macmillan failed to show the same courage that had led them to ignore similar veiled threats from Shapley; they passed on Velikovsky to the Doubleday corporation, who had no textbook department to worry about, and who were probably unable to believe their luck in being handed such a profitable piece of intellectual merchandise. Fred Whipple, Shapley's successor at Harvard, wrote to Doubleday[1] telling them that if they persisted in publishing Velikovsky, he wanted them to take his own book *Earth, Moon and Planets* off their list. (Twenty years later, he denied in print ever writing such a letter.)

Velikovsky himself was rather bewildered by the sheer violence of the reactions; it had taken him thirty years to develop his theory, and he had expected controversy; but this amounted to persecution. He was willing to admit that he could be wrong about the nature of the catastrophe; but the historical records showed that *something* had taken place. Why couldn't they admit that, and *then* criticize his theory,

---

1. In fact, to the Doubleday subsidiary, Blakiston.

instead of treating him as a madman? The only thing to do was to go on collecting more evidence.

And more evidence was produced in intimidating quantities during the remaining twenty-nine years of Velikovsky's life; he died on 17 November 1979, at the age of eighty-four. In 1955 came *Earth in Upheaval*, in many ways his best book, presenting the scientific evidence for great catastrophes. But again it outraged scientists – this time biologists – by suggesting that there are serious inadequacies in Darwin's theory of "gradual evolution", and arguing that a better explanation would be the effect of radiation due to "catastrophes" on the genes. Then came four books in a series that Velikovsky chose to call *Ages in Chaos*, whose main thesis is that historians of the ancient world have made a basic mistake in their dating, and that a period of about six or seven centuries needs to be dropped from the chronological record. In Velikovsky's dating, Queen Hatshepsut, generally assumed to have lived about 1500 BC, becomes a contemporary of Solomon more than four centuries later (in fact, Velikovsky identifies her with the Queen of Sheba), while the pharaoh Rameses II assumed to live around 1250 BC becomes a contemporary of Nebuchadnezzar more than six centuries later. The great invasion of barbarians known as the Sea Peoples, usually dated about 1200 BC, is placed by Velikovsky in the middle of the fourth century BC, about the time of the death of Plato. The arguments contained in *Ages in Chaos* (1953), *Oedipus and Akhnaton* (1960), *Peoples of the Sea* (1977) and *Rameses II and his Time* (1978) are of interest to historians rather than to scientists, but, like the earlier works, are totally absorbing to read. Two other projected volumes, *The Dark Age in Greece* and *The Assyrian Conquest*, have not so far been published. But a third volume of the *Worlds in Collision* series, *Mankind in Amnesia*, appeared posthumously in 1982. It expands a short section in *Worlds in Collision* arguing that catastrophic events produce a kind of collective amnesia. It is his most Freudian book, but it reveals that he

141

never lost that curious ability to produce a state of intellectual excitement in the reader, even when his arguments seem most outrageous.

How far does Velikovsky deserve to be taken seriously? Should he be regarded as another Freud, or merely as another Erich von Däniken? It must be admitted that the basic thesis of *Worlds in Collision* sounds preposterous: that various Biblical events, like the parting of the Red Sea and the fall of the walls of Jericho, can be explained in terms of an astronomical catastrophe. But it is possible to entertain doubts about this aspect of Velikovsky's thesis without dismissing the most important part of his theory: that Venus may be far younger than the rest of the solar system. Moreover, whether or not Velikovsky is correct about the origin of Venus, there can be no doubt whatever that many of his controversial insights have been confirmed. Astronomers object that Jupiter was not likely to be the source of a "comet" because it is too cold and inactive. However, a standard textbook of astronomy – Skilling and Richardson (1947) – states "From the fact that Jupiter is 5.2 times as far from the source of heat as is the earth, it can be seen that it should receive only $1/5.2^2$, or $1/27$ as much heat as does the earth. The temperature that a planet should have as the result of this much heat is very low – in the neighbourhood of $-140°C$." But space probes have since revealed that the surface temperature on Jupiter is around $-150°C$, and that its surface is extremely turbulent, with immense explosions. The same textbook of astronomy states that the temperature on the surface of Venus "may be as high as boiling water". Velikovsky argued that it should be much higher, since Venus is so "young" in astronomical terms. Mariner 2 revealed that the temperature on the surface of Venus is about $900°C$. It also revealed the curious fact that Venus rotates backwards as compared to all the other planets, an oddity that seems incomprehensible if it was formed at the same time and evolved through the same process.

Russian space probes also revealed that Venus has violent electrical storms. Velikovsky had argued that the planets have powerful magnetic fields, and that therefore a close brush between the earth and a "comet" would produce quite definite effects. The discovery of the Van Allen belts around the earth supported Velikovsky's view. There also seem to be close links between the rotation of Venus and Earth – Venus turns the same face to earth at each inferior conjunction, which could have come about through an interlocking of their magnetic fields. In the 1950s Velikovsky's assertion about electromagnetic fields in space was treated with contempt – in *Fads and Fallacies in the Name of Science*, Martin Gardner remarked dismissively that Velikovsky had invented forces capable of doing whatever he wanted them to do. His electromagnetic theory also led Velikovsky to predict that Jupiter would be found to emit radio waves, and that the sun would have an extremely powerful magnetic field. One critic (D. Menzel) retorted that Velikovsky's model of the sun would require an impossible charge of 10^{19} volts. Since then, Jupiter has been found to emit radio waves, while the sun's electrical potential has been calculated at about 10^{19} volts. It could be said that many of Velikovsky's theories are now an accepted part of astrophysics except, of course, that no one acknowledges that Velikovsky was the first one to formulate them.

Another matter on which Velikovsky seems to have been proved correct is the question of the reversal of the earth's magnetic poles. When molten volcanic rocks cool, or when clay or brick is baked, the magnetic minerals in it are magnetized in the direction of the earth's magnetic field. At the turn of the century Giuseppe Folgerhaiter examined Etruscan vases, looking for minor magnetic variations, and was astonished to find that there seemed to have been a complete reversal of the magnetic field around the eighth century BC. Scientists explained his findings by declaring that the pots must have been fired upside down. But in 1906 Bernard Brunhes found the same complete reversal in certain volcanic rocks. Further research revealed that there had been at least nine such reversals in the past 3.6 million years. No one could make any plausible suggestion as to why this had happened. Velikovsky's suggestion was that it was due to the close approach of other celestial bodies, and that the earth's brush with Venus should have produced such a reversal. His critics replied that there have been no reversals in the past half-million years or so. But since then two more have been discovered – one 28,000 years ago, the other about 12500 BC – and one of Velikovsky's bitterest opponents, Harold Urey, has come to admit that the "celestial body" theory is the likeliest explanation of pole-reversal. Yet so far the crucial piece of evidence – volcanic rock revealing a reversal about 1450 BC – has not been forthcoming.

Those who regard Velikovsky as an innovator comparable to Freud should also be prepared to admit that he had many of Freud's faults – particularly a tendency to jump to bold and unorthodox conclusions, and then to stick by them with a certain rigid dogmatism. Yet it must also be admitted that whether or not his Venus theory proves to be ultimately correct, his "guesses" have often been amazingly accurate. Like Kepler, who came to all the right conclusions about the solar system for all the wrong reasons (including the belief that it is somehow modelled on the Holy Trinity), Velikovsky seems to possess the intuitive genius of all great innovators. Even one of his most dismissive critics, Carl Sagan, admits: "I find the concatenation of legends which Velikovsky has accumulated stunning . . . If twenty per cent of the legendary concordances . . . are real, there is something important to be explained."

Chapter Eighteen

"The Most Mysterious Manuscript in the World"

The Voynich Manuscript

It was in 1912 that an American dealer in rare books, Wilfred Voynich, heard of a mysterious work that had been discovered in an old chest in the Jesuit school of Mondragone, in Frascati, Italy, and succeeded in buying it for an undisclosed sum. It was an octavo volume, six by nine inches, with 204 pages; it had originally another 28 pages, but these are lost. It is written in cipher, which at first glance looks like ordinary medieval writing. And the pages are covered with strange little drawings of female nudes, astronomical diagrams, and all kinds of strange plants in many colours.

There was a letter accompanying the manuscript, dated 19 August 1666, and written by Joannes Marcus Marci, the rector of Prague University. It was addressed to the famous Jesuit scholar Athanasius Kircher – remembered today mainly for some interesting experiments in animal hypnosis – and stated that the book had been bought for 600 ducats by the Holy Roman Emperor Rudolf II of Prague. Kircher was an expert on cryptography, having published a book on the subject in 1663, in which he claimed to have solved the riddle of hieroglyphics. This in itself may be taken to indicate that Kircher was inclined to indulge in wishful thinking, since we know that it would be another century and a half before Champollion succeeded in reading hieroglyphics. Kircher had apparently already attempted to decipher a few pages of the book, sent to him by its previous owner, who had devoted his whole life to trying to decode it. Now he sent him the whole manuscript.

We do not know how the manuscript came to be in Prague, but the likeliest possibility is that it was taken there from England by the famous Elizabethan "magician" Dr John Dee, who went there in 1584; one writer speculates that Dee may have obtained it from the Duke of Northumberland, who had pillaged monasteries at the behest of Henry VIII. The English writer Sir Thomas Browne said later that Dee's son Arthur had spoken about "a book containing nothing but hieroglyphics" which he had studied in Prague. Marci believed the mysterious book to be by the thirteenth-century monk and scientist Roger Bacon.

The Voynich manuscript (as it came to be known) is a baffling mystery because it looks so straightforward; with its drawings of plants it looks like an ordinary medieval

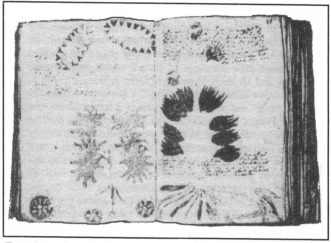

Two pages from the Voynich manuscript. For years cryptologists have tried to unravel its secrets – without success.

"herbal", a book describing how to extract healing drugs from plants. One would expect astronomical or astrological diagrams in a herbal, because the plants were often supposed to be gathered by the full moon, or when the stars or planets were in a certain position.

Kircher obviously had no success with the manuscript; he finally deposited it in the Jesuit College in Rome, whence it came into the hands of the Jesuits of Frascati.

Voynich was fairly certain that the manuscript would not remain a mystery once modern scholars had a chance to study it. So he distributed photostats to anyone who was interested. The first problem, of course, was to determine what language it was in – Latin, Middle English, perhaps even Langue d'Oc. This should have been an easy task, since the plants were labelled, albeit in some sort of code. But most of the plants proved to be imaginary. Certain constellations could be recognized among the astronomical diagrams but again, it proved impossible to translate their names out of code. Cryptanalysts tried the familiar method of looking for the most frequent symbols and equating them with the most commonly used letters of the alphabet; they had no difficulty recognizing twenty-nine individual letters or symbols, but every attempt to translate these into a known language was a failure. What made it so infuriating was that the writing didn't *look* like a code; it looked as if someone had sat down and written it as fluently as his mother tongue. Many scholars, cryptanalysts, linguists, astronomers, experts on Bacon, offered to help; the Vatican Library offered to throw open its archives to the researchers. Still the manuscript refused to yield up its secret – or even one of its secrets.

Then in 1921 a professor of philosophy from the University of Pennsylvania, William Romaine Newbold, announced that he had solved the code; he explained his discovery before a meeting of the American Philosophical Society in Philadelphia. What he had done, he explained, was to start by translating the symbols into Roman letters, reducing them in the process from twenty-nine to seventeen. Using the Latin *conmuto* (or *commuto*: to change) as a key word, he then went on to produce no less than four more versions of the text, the last of which was (according to Newbold) a straightforward Latin text mixed up into anagrams. These merely had to be unscrambled and the result was a scientific treatise which revealed that Roger Bacon was one of the greatest intellects of all time.

This had, of course, always been suspected. It was Bacon who had inspired Columbus to seek out America by a passage in his *Opus Majus* in which he suggested that the Indies could be reached by sailing westward from Spain. In the days of alchemy and a dogmatic and muddled science derived from Aristotle, Bacon advocated learning from nature by experiment and observation, and was thrown into prison for his pains. In rejecting the authority of Aristotle he was also by implication rejecting the authority of the Church. In his *City of God*, St Augustine had warned Christians to shun science and intellectual inquiry as a danger to salvation. Roger Bacon, like his Elizabethan namesake Francis, could see that such an attitude was tantamount to intellectual suicide. Yet when all this is said, it has to be admitted that Bacon was very much a man of his time, and that the *Opus Majus* is full of statements that a modern scientist would regard as gross errors and superstitions.

But if Newbold was correct, Bacon was one of the greatest scientists before Newton. He had made a microscope and examined biological cells and spermatozoa – these were the tadpole-drawings in the margins – and had made a telescope long before Galileo; he had even recognized the Andromeda nebula as a spiral galaxy. Newbold translated a caption to what he claimed to be a sketch of the nebula: "In a concave mirror I saw a star in the form of a snail . . . between the navel of Pegasus, the girdle of Andromeda and the head of Cassiopeia." (It is known that Bacon understood how to use a concave mirror as a burning-glass.) Newbold declared that he had no idea of what he would find by looking in the region indicated, and was surprised to find that the "snail" was the Andromeda nebula.

But in *The Codebreakers* cipher expert David Kahn has pointed out one of the basic flaws in Newbold's system. Newbold's method depended on "doubling up" the letters of a word, so that, for example, "oritur" became or-ri-it-tu-ur, and this text was solved with the aid of the key word "conmuto" and the addition of a q. But how would this process be carried out in reverse – in other words, when Bacon was turning his original text into a cipher? Kahn says: "Many one-way ciphers have been devised; it is possible to put messages into cipher, but not to get them back out. Newbold's seemed to be the only example extant of the reverse situation."

Newbold died in 1926, only sixty years old; two years later his friend Roland G. Kent published the results of Newbold's labours in *The Cipher of Roger Bacon*. It was widely accepted – for example, by the eminent cultural historian Étienne Gilson.

But one scholar who had been studying Newbold's system was far from convinced. He was Dr John M. Manly, a philologist who headed the department of English at Chicago University, and who had become assistant to the great Herbert Osborne Yardley – described as the greatest codebreaker in history – when US Military Intelligence set up a cryptanalysis department in 1917. Manly had produced the definitive edition of Chaucer in eight volumes, comparing more than eighty versions of the medieval manuscript of the *Canterbury Tales*. One of his most remarkable feats was the deciphering of a letter found in the baggage of a German spy named Lothar Witzke, who was captured in Nogales, Mexico, in 1918. In three days of non-stop application Manly had solved the twelve-step official transposition cipher, with multiple horizontal shiftings of three and four letter groups finally laid out in a vertical transcription. In a military court he was able to read aloud a message from the German minister in Mexico beginning: "The bearer of this is a subject of the empire who travels as a Russian under the name of Pablo Waberski. He is a German secret agent . . ." It was the spy's death warrant (although President Wilson commuted it to life imprisonment).

Now Manly studied Newbold's *Cipher of Roger Bacon,* and concluded that in spite of his undoubted integrity, Newbold had been deceiving himself. The weak point of the cipher was the anagramming process. Most sentences can be anagrammed into a dozen other sentences, a method by which admirers of Francis Bacon have had no difficulty proving that he wrote the plays of Shakespeare. With a sentence involving more than a hundred letters, there is simply no way of guaranteeing that some particular rearrangement provides the only solution – David Kahn points out that the words "Hail Mary, full of grace, the Lord is with thee" can be anagrammed in thousands of different ways.

Newbold had also made certain "shorthand signs" a basic part of his system of interpretation. When Manly looked at these through a powerful magnifying glass he found out that they were not "shorthand" at all, only places where the ink had peeled off the vellum. By the time he had pointed out dozens of cases in which Newbold had allowed his interpretation to be influenced by his own twentieth-century assumptions, Manly had totally demolished Newbold's claim to have solved "the cipher of Roger Bacon".

Since that time, 1931, there have been many attempts to decipher the Voynich manuscript. In 1933 a cancer specialist, Dr Leonell C. Strong, published his own fragments of translation, and proved to his own satisfaction that the work was a herbal by an English scholar, Anthony Ascham; he even published a recipe for a contraceptive which apparently works. But Strong failed to explain the method by which he arrived at his translations, so they have never achieved wide acceptance.

William F. Friedman, who organized a whole group of specialists to work on the problem in the last year of World War II, was frustrated by the end of the war and the disbandment of his group. But Friedman pointed out that the Voynich manuscript differs from other codes in one basic respect. The inventor of a code attempts to frustrate would-be cryptanalysts by trying to remove repetitions that would give him away (for example, a repeated group of three words would almost certainly be "and" or "the"). The Voynich manuscript actually has far more repetitions than an ordinary text. This led Friedman to hypothesize that the text is in some artificial language which, because of a need for simplicity, would inevitably have more repetitions than a highly complex "natural" language. But this presupposes that Roger Bacon (or whoever wrote the manuscript) was so anxious to conceal his meanmg that he went to far greater lengths than even a code-expert would consider reasonable. And for a thirteenth-century monk, who had little reason to fear code-breakers, this seems unlikely . . .

And this, of course, is the very heart of the mystery. We do not know when the manuscript was written, or by whom, or in what language, but even if we knew the answers to these questions it is difficult to think of any good reason for inventing such a baffling code. The earliest ciphers in the Vatican archive date from 1326 (when Roger Bacon was a boy) and these are merely "coded" names relating to the struggle between Ghibellines and Guelphs. These were respectively supporters of the Holy Roman Emperor and the Pope; the Ghibellines are called Egyptians and the Guelphs Children of Israel. (It is easy to guess what side the inventor of the code was on.) The earliest Western "substitution" cipher dates from 1401. The first treatise on codes, the *Polygraphia* of Johannes Trithemius, was not printed until 1518, two years after the death of its author. So it is hard to imagine why Roger Bacon or anyone within a century of his death should have gone to so much trouble to invent a code of such apparent sophistication when something much simpler would have sufficed.

Kahn offers one clue to why the author of a herbal (which is what the Voynich manuscript looks most like) should want to conceal his meaning when he speaks of one of the earliest encipherments, a tiny cuneiform tablet dating from about 1500 BC. "It contains the earliest known formula for the making of glazes for pottery. The scribe, jealously guarding his professional secret, used cuneiform signs . . . in their least common values." The author of the Voynich manuscript may have been a highly skilled professional herbalist who wrote down his secrets for his own use and those of his pupils, and was determined to keep them out of the hands of rivals.

This view would have struck the antiquarian bookseller Hans Kraus as altogether too commonplace. When Ethel Voynich died at the age of ninety-six, in 1960, Kraus purchased the manuscript from her executors and put it up for sale at $160,000; he explained that he thought that it could contain information that might provide new insights into the record of man, and that if it could be deciphered it might be worth a million dollars. No one took it at that price, and Kraus finally gave it to Yale University in 1969, where it now lies, awaiting the inspiration of some master-cryptographer.

Chapter Ninteen

Crop Circles – UFOs, Whirlwinds or Hoaxers?

On 15 August 1980, the *Wiltshire Times* carried an odd report concerning apparently wanton vandalism of a field of oats near Westbury in Wiltshire. The owner of the field, John Scull, had found his oats crushed to the ground in three separate areas all within sight of the famous White Horse of Westbury, the hillside figure cut into the chalk. It seemed obvious to Scull that the crops had been damaged by people rather than natural phenomena, since the areas were identical in size and shape; almost perfect circles, sixty feet in diameter.

It was noted that the circles had apparently been produced manually rather than mechanically, since there was no sign that any kind of machinery had been moved through the field. In fact there seemed to be no evidence of *anything* crossing the field; the circles were surrounded by undamaged oats, with no paths that would indicate intruders. One speculation was that the vandals had used stilts.

Close examination of the flattened cereal revealed that all the circles had not been made at the same time – in fact, that the damage had been spread over a period of two or three months, probably between May and the end of July. The edges to the circles were sharply defined, and all the grain within the circle was flattened in the same direction, creating a clockwise swirling effect around the centre. None of the oats had been cut – merely flattened. The effect might have been produced by a very tall and strong man standing in the centre and swinging a heavy weight around on a long piece of rope . . .

Strange Tales and Weird Mysteries

Dr Terence Meaden, an atmospheric physicist from nearby Bradford-on-Avon – and a senior member of the Tornado and Storm Research Organization (TORRO) – suggested that the effect had been produced by a summer whirlwind. Such wind effects are not uncommon on open farmland. But Dr Meaden had to admit that he had never seen or heard of a whirlwind creating exact circles. Whirlwinds tend to scud about randomly, pausing for only a few seconds in any one place – so one might expect a random pathway through the crop with only occasionally wider areas of damage to fields.

Another interesting fact was also noted by Ian Mrzyglod, editor of the anomaly magazine *The PROBE Report*. The "centre point" on all three circles was in fact off centre by as much as four feet. The swirling patterns around them were therefore oval, not circular. This seemed to contradict the vandal theory – vandals would hardly go to the trouble of creating precise ellipses. It also made Meaden's whirlwind explanation seem less plausible.

Almost exactly a year later on 19 August 1981, another three-circle formation appeared in wheat below Cheesefoot Head, near Winchester in Hampshire. These circles had been created at the same time and, unlike the widely dispersed circles in Wiltshire, were in close formation – one circle sixty feet across with two twenty-five-foot circles on either side. The sides of the circles had the same precise edges, and again the swirl of the flattened plants was slightly off centre, creating an ellipse. Again there were no paths through the corn to indicate intruders.

The new evidence seemed to undermine the natural causes theory. Instead of a neat, stationary whirlwind creating only one circle, Meaden now had to argue the existence of an atmospheric disturbance that "hopscotched" across the land-scape, and produced circles of different sizes – instead of the identical ones that might be expected from a whirlwind. Meaden suggested that perhaps peculiarities of terrain created this effect – the field in question was on a concave,

154

"punchbowl" slope and this might indeed have caused the vortex to "jump".

There were a few isolated reports of incidents in 1982, but they were unspectacular and excited little attention. As if to make up for it, a series of five-circle phenomena began in 1983, one of them again at Bratton, close to the White Horse of Westbury. These made it clear that whirlwinds could not explain the circles, for they consisted of one large circle with four smaller ones spaced around it like the number 5 on a dice. More "quintuplets" appeared at Cley Hill, near Warminster – a town that, in earlier years, had had more than its share of "Flying Saucer" sightings – and in a field below Ridgeway near Wantage in Oxfordshire. Quintuplets were no longer freaks, but were virtually the norm.

Now the national press began to cover the phenomena. The British press often refer to the summer as the "silly season" because – for some odd reason – there is often a shortage of good news stories in the hot months of the year, so newspapers tend to supply the deficiency by blowing up trivia into major news stories. Crop circles answered the need perfectly, with the result that the British public soon became familiar with the strange circle formations. UFO enthusiasts appeared on television explaining their view that the phenomena could only be explained by Flying Saucers. Sceptics preferred the notion of fraud.

This view seemed to be confirmed when a second "quintuplet" found at Bratton turned out to be a hoax sponsored by the *Daily Mirror*; a family called Shepherd had been paid to duplicate the other Bratton circles. They did this by entering the field upon stilts and trampling the crops underfoot. But, significantly, the hoax was quickly detected by the editor of an anomaly magazine, *The Fortean Times*, Bob Rickard, who noted the tell-tale signs of human intruders which had not been present in earlier circles, and the fact that the edges of the circles were so rough and imprecise. The aim of the hoax was to embarrass the competing tabloid the *Daily*

Express, which had originally scooped the crop circle story.

During the next two years the number of circles increased, as did their complexity. There were crop circles with "rings" around them – flattened pathways several feet wide, that ran around the outer edge in a neat circle – some were even found with two or three such parameters. At the same time the quintuplet formations and "singletons" also continued to appear.

It began to look as if whoever – or whatever – was creating the circles took pleasure in taunting the investigators. When believers in the whirlwind theory pointed out the "swirling" had so far been clockwise, a circle promptly appeared that was anti-clockwise. When it was suggested that a hoaxer might be making the circles with the use of a helicopter, a crop circle was found directly beneath a power line. And when an aerial photographer named Busty Taylor was flying home after photographing crop circles, and mentioned that he would like to see a formation in the shape of a celtic cross, a celtic cross appeared the next day in the field they had been flying over. And, as if to rule out all possibility that natural causes could be responsible, one "sextuplet" in Hampshire in 1990 had key-like objects sticking out of the sides of three circles, producing an impression like ancient pictograms. Another crop "pattern" of 1990 (at Chilcomb) seemed to represent a kind of chemical retort with a long neck, with four rectangles neatly spaced on either side of it, making nonsense of Meaden's insistence that the circles are caused by "natural atmospheric forces".

Rickard brought together a number of eyewitness descriptions of the actual appearance of circles.

"Suddenly the grass began to sway before our eyes and laid itself flat in a clockwise spiral . . . A perfect circle was completed in less than half a minute, all the time accompanied by a high-pitched humming sound . . . My attention was drawn to a wave coming through the heads of the cereal crop in a straight line . . . The agency, though invisible, behaved like a solid object . . . When we reached the spot where the circles had been, we were suddenly caught up in a terrific whirlwind . . . [The dog] went wild . . . There was a rushing sound and a rumble . . . then suddenly everything was still . . . It was uncanny . . . The dawn chorus stopped; the sky darkened . . ."

The high-pitched humming sound may be significant. It was noted on another occasion, on 16 June 1991, when a seventy-five-foot circle (with a "bullseye" at the centre) appeared on Bolberry Down, near Salcombe in Devon. A local radio ham named Lew Dilling was tuned into a regular frequency when strange high-pitched bips and clicks emerged. He recognized the sounds as the same as others that had been heard in connection with other crop circle incidents. "The signals were so powerful," said Dilling, "that you could hear them in the background of Radio Moscow and Voice of America – and they would normally swamp everything."

The landlord of the local pub, Sean Hassall, learned of the crop circle indirectly when his spaniel went berserk and began tearing up the carpet, doing considerable damage.

The farmer, Dudley Stidson, was alerted to the circle by two walkers. He went to the six-acre hay field and found the huge circle in the centre. But this one differed from many such circles in that the hay was burnt, as if someone had put a huge hot-ring on it. Stidson emphasized that there was no sign of intrusion in the field, such as trampled wheat.

Another local farmer, Peter Goodall, found a sixty-foot circle in his winter wheat (at Matford Barton) at the same time.

A few days before these incidents, a Japanese professor had announced that he had solved the crop circle mystery. Professor Yoshihiko Ohtsuki, of Tokyo's Waseda University, had created an "elastic plasma" fireball – a very strong form of ionized air – in the laboratory. When the fireball touched a plate covered with aluminium powder, it created beautiful circles and rings in the powder. Ohtsuki suggested that plasma fireballs are created by atmospheric conditions, and that they would flatten the crops as they descended towards the ground. This certainly sounds as if it could be the solution of the mystery – until we remember the crop circles with rectangles, or key-like objects sticking out of the side. Another objection is that fireballs are usually about the size of footballs, and are clearly visible. Surely a fireball with a seventy-five-foot diameter would be visible for many miles? And why were no fireballs seen by witnesses cited by Rickard, who simply saw the corn being flattened in a clock-wise circle?

Another recent suggestion is that an excess of fertilizer will cause the corn to shoot up much faster than that which surrounds it, but that it then "collapses" and lies flat. Here there are two objections: why a farmer should spray an excess of fertilizer in a circle – or some even more complicated design – and why the corn should "collapse" in a clockwise direction . . .

In a symposium called *The Crop Circle Enigma* (1990), John Michell has made the important suggestion that the crop circles have a meaning, and that "the meaning . . . is to be found in the way people are affected by them". He goes on: "Jung discerned the meaning of UFOs as agents and portents of changes in human thought patterns, and that function has been clearly inherited by crop circles."

In order to understand this fully, we have to bear in mind Jung's concept of "synchronicity" or "meaningful coincidence". His view is basically that "meaningful coin-cidences" are somehow *created* by the unconscious mind – probably with the intention of jarring the conscious mind into a keener state of perception. Preposterous synchron-icities imbue us with a powerful sense that there is a hidden meaning behind everyday reality. Certain pessimistically inclined writers – such as Shakespeare and Thomas Hardy – have taken the view that accidents and disasters indicate a kind of malevolent intelligence behind life. Jung's view is that synchronicities produce a sense of a benevolent intelligence behind life. He suggested at one point that the UFO phenomenon was an example of what he called "projection" that is, of a physical effect somehow produced by the unconscious mind – in fact, by the "collective unconscious".

What Michell is suggesting, in effect, is that the crop circle phenomenon has the same purpose. Yet to say, as he does, that the crop circles have a "meaning" could also imply that some "other intelligence" is trying to influence human thought patterns. This is an idea that has been current since the earliest UFO sightings in the late 1940s, and was popularized by Arthur C. Clarke in the film script of *2001 A Space Odyssey*: the notion that "higher intelligences" have been involved in the evolution of the human brain.

The logical objection to this is that to "make" man evolve is a contradiction in terms; evolution is due to an *inner* drive. Presumably a higher intelligence would recognize this better than we do. Yet it is also true that intelligence evolves through a sense of curiosity, of mystery, and that such apparent absurdities as flying saucers and crop circles certainly qualify as mysteries.

Michell concludes by quoting Jung's words that UFOs are "signs of great changes to come which are compatible with the end of an era". And whether or not Jung was correct, there can be no doubt that the UFO phenomenon has played an enormous part in the transformation of human consciousness from the narrow scientific materialism of the first half of the twentieth century to the far more open-minded attitude of its second half. Whether or not they prove to have a "natural" explanation, this may be the ultimate significance of the crop circles in the history of the late twentieth century.

In 1992, two men confessed to having made the crop circles as a hoax, using a long board on a pivot. Most experts have dismissed this as a possible explanation – the difference between genuine circles and hoaxes being fairly easy to detect. Even if some circles had been made by the two hoaxers, it would have been impossible for two men to have made all of them. Tests to be conducted by zoologist Rupert Sheldrake – who has offered a prize for the best "fake" crop circle – may throw further light on the problem. For the moment, it remains stubbornly intractable.

Crop Circles – UFOs, Whirlwinds or Hoaxers?

On the night of 18 April 1962 at about 7.30 p.m. an explosion ripped across the Nevada sky. The flash was as bright as an atomic blast, and the noise shook the earth for miles. Was it an atom bomb test? A meteor? An enemy missile or aircraft? These logical questions were never answered by those who investigated the incident.

The first report of an odd UFO had come from Oneida, New York. Observers there saw a glowing red object moving west at a great altitude. It was too slow to be a missile, too high to be a plane. A meteor was ruled out because this object was tracked by radar, and meteors cannot be. As it moved west across the country, reports of it came in from the states of Kansas, Utah, Montana, New Mexico, Wyoming, Arizona, and California.

At some point the huge UFO landed near an electric power station in Eureka, Utah. Until it took off again, in its own time, the station was unable to operate at all.

The possibility that the explosion was from a nuclear test was denied by the Atomic Energy Commission. Its spokesmen said there was no atomic testing anywhere on the North American continent at that time.

Jet interceptors from the Air Defense Command pursued the UFO, but radar screens lost it about seventy miles northwest of Las Vegas. It was in that precise direction that the blast took place somewhere above the Mesquite Range.

Few people in the United States ever learned about this unusual event. Only the Las Vegas *Sun*, which was in the area of the explosion, carried the story. The news was otherwise suppressed by the Air Force.

Chapter Twenty

The Disappearance of the Vaughan Children

O n a warm June Sunday in 1906, a youth named Harold Wilkins was asked to join a search party for three missing children. That morning, the three had gone to play in a field near their home, a mile from Gloucester – a boy, aged ten, and his two sisters, aged three and five. When they failed to return home for lunch, their father, a railway brakeman named Vaughan, went to look for them in "Forty Acre" field; he found no sign of them, so he raised the alarm, and crowds of neighbours searched the area and the surrounding countryside.

M ore than half a century later, Harold Wilkins told the story in a book called *Mysteries, Solved and Unsolved*: how he and many others had scoured the field, which was close to the locomotive-engine shed of the old Midland Railway, and had failed to find the slightest sign of the children. "Every inch was probed with sticks . . . Had a dead dog been dumped there, he would certainly have been found." The police came to the conclusion that the Vaughan children had been kidnapped, and the following morning newspapers were full of the story. The Vaughan family received a great deal of sympathy, and cash donations and postal orders began to pour into the local post office. Vaughan himself seems to have been a rather coarse and brutal character, who when the local vicar called, closed the door in his face with the comment that he "didn't want no bloody parsons knocking at his door".

At 6 a.m. on the following Thursday morning, a ploughman starting work in a nearby field looked over a hedge and saw the three children fast asleep in a ditch. They were quickly restored to their parents, and newspaper readers awaited the solution of the mystery with interest. They were disappointed. The children had no idea of what all the fuss was about, and no idea that they had been missing for three days. The Superintendent of the Gloucester police, Nehemiah Philpott, took the view that the ploughman had kidnapped the children for ransom, and the children's father had refused to hand over a penny of the reward money, which had been donated by readers of the *News of the World*. But local reporters only had to look at the labourer's cottage – in the nearby hamlet of Coney Hill – to see that this could not be true; it was tiny, and so close to neighbouring cottages that it would have been impossible to smuggle a cat in without being noticed. Besides, the ploughman had been gathering in the harvest at the time the children had vanished.

When Wilkins told the story in 1959, the eldest of the missing children was still alive, and verified that he did not have the slightest recollection of what happened in the four days during which hundreds of people were searching. It is true that the ditch where they were found might have been overlooked. But would three children sleep straight through four days?

Wilkins has his own theory about the mystery. He suggests that certain places on earth – places associated with witchcraft and ancient rites – are pervaded by strange unknown forces, and that such forces may not be limited by our normal space-time dimensions. But whether or not we can accept the "strange forces" theory, the fact remains that there have been hundreds of similar "vanishings" – so many that whole books have been devoted to them. And many cases involve people who have disappeared "into thin air".

Walter Powell was an English politician who was the Member of Parliament for a Wiltshire area. On 1 December 1881 he became part of an unsolved mystery when he went up in a balloon with two of his friends. They came down on a beach in Dorset, the two got out, and Powell started to follow. Suddenly the balloon gave a violent jerk and went high up into the clouds again with Powell still on board. He was never seen again.

It seemed likely that he might have crashed into the English Channel, and a search was made for three days. The beaches on England's southern coast were combed for clues night and day. Nothing helpful turned up anywhere.

Right after Powell's disappearance, reports of mystifying lights and objects in the sky came from England, France, Scotland, and Spain. The day after Powell and the balloon had vanished, people in Dartmouth Harbour saw "two strange bright lights in the sky". Two days later an unidentified luminous object was seen traversing the sky over Cherbourg, France.

On 15 December a ship's captain saw a glowing object in the sky. He described it as the "gondola of a balloon, which seemed alternately to increase and diminish in size". That was in the east of Scotland. On the 16th, three Spanish coastguards reported seeing something that looked like a balloon in the sky. They climbed the nearby mountain to investigate, and saw it shoot out sparks as it vanished. The next day about seventy-five miles east of this sighting, a similar and strangely glowing object was reported.

Could these unusual sightings have had a connection with Powell's lost balloon?

Chapter Twenty-One

The Missing Army

In April 1915 Allied armies landed on the Gallipoli Peninsula in European Turkey in an attempt to capture what was then the capital of the Turkish Empire (now Istanbul). They wanted to make contact with Russian allies through the Black Sea. It was bad strategy. Turkish resistance was stubborn, and the Allies were forced to withdraw nine months later, having lost hundreds of thousands of men.

Some of the bloodiest fighting in Gallipoli took place around a spot called Hill 60 near Suvla Bay. On the morning of 28 August 1915 a British regiment, the First Fourth Norfolk, prepared to attack Hill 60. The regiment consisted of more than a thousand men. It was a warm, clear day, but several observers remember noticing a group of curious low clouds over Hill 60. Although there was a breeze, these clouds seemed to remain stationary. The observers reported watching the regiment march uphill until the entire file of men disappeared into one of these "loaf-shaped" clouds. Then the clouds moved away – leaving no sign of the army.

The disappearance of the regiment was duly reported to the British Government by the Commander-in-Chief of the Allied Expeditionary Force in Gallipoli. He made no mention of the mysterious clouds, but reported that the regiment had separated from the main body of troops and had vanished. The whole regiment was subsequently posted as "missing" – the assumption being that all its men had either been killed or taken prisoner. When the war ended in 1918 the British asked the Turks about their missing regiment. The Turks replied that they knew nothing about it. Their armies had never made contact with the First Fourth Norfolk.

Strange Tales and Weird Mysteries

In 1920 the bodies of a number of soldiers belonging to the First Fourth Norfolk were found in Gallipoli. It was assumed that these men must have died in battle after all, and that the remainder of the regiment probably perished in Turkish prisoner-of-war camps. Today it is generally accepted that the men of the First Fourth Norfolk were victims of a bloody campaign in which all too many men were lost without trace.

Some people, however, have never accepted this explanation – particularly the witnesses who recalled the strange clouds over Hill 60. The French writer Jacques Vallée was sufficiently curious to investigate the matter, and included the incident in his book *Passport to Magonia*. He used a letter signed by three witnesses attesting to the curious disappearance of the whole regiment into a cloud.

Vallée is a scientist connected with Northwestern University in Chicago. He has also written one of the most balanced books on Unidentified Flying Objects, *Anatomy of a phenomenon*. Vallée puts forward the idea that the regiment marched into a cloud that concealed a UFO. This view is supported by the distinguished British ufologist Brinsley Le Poer Trench, now the Earl of Clancarty, who is Chairman of the International UFO Movement. Le Poer Trench cites another cloud disappearance in the curious case of Dr and Mrs Gerardo Vidal. They were driving home from a family reunion in Chascomus, Argentina, when they drove into a thick cloud of mist. They fell unconscious – and woke to find themselves on a road near Mexico City, 4,500 miles away. On telephoning friends in Argentina, they discovered that they had apparently lost two days since they left the party.

Chapter Twenty-Two

Caspar Hauser

The most famous case of a strange person appearing in mysterious circumstances is that of Caspar Hauser. On 26 May 1828 a shambling teenage boy wandered into the Unschlitt Square in Nuremberg, Germany. Trembling and mumbling incoherently, he accosted a shoemaker and offered him a letter. When he was taken to the police station, another letter was found in his pocket. One letter purported to be from his mother, who said that the boy's name was Caspar, and that his father had been a soldier. The other was apparently from a poor labourer who had brought up the boy, and who asked that he be taken into the army. It was quickly established that both letters were fakes, written by the same person probably to cover up the boy's identity.

Asked to write his name, the boy wrote "Caspar Hauser". He was able to mumble a few words, but otherwise gave the impression of being imbecilic. It soon became clear, however, that Hauser was not an imbecile. Although he seemed totally ignorant of the world and of even the most everyday objects in it, he began to learn with a rapidity that proved he was highly intelligent. Within a few months, Caspar Hauser had learned enough German to explain what he knew of his former life. He said that for as long as he could recall, he had lived in a tiny cell. When he awoke, he found bread and water on the floor. Sometimes the water tasted bitter, and after drinking it he fell into a deep sleep. When he woke up, he had been washed and his nails had been cut. He was not unhappy because he knew no other way of life.

Handbills were sent out all over Germany to try to establish the boy's identity, but no one was able to throw any light on the mystery. Professor Georg Daumer, who became Hauser's guardian, discovered that the boy had an unusually acute sense of smell, could see in the dark, and found daylight painful to his eyes – all of which seemed to confirm his story.

In October 1829 Hauser was found unconscious and bleeding on the floor of Daumer's cellar. He had been attacked by an unknown assailant who had struck him down with a club, and possibly also tried to stab him.

During the next four years, Hauser had a number of guardians. Finally an Englishman, Lord Charles Stanhope, moved him from Nuremberg to the nearby town of Ansbach in Bavaria. On 14 December 1833 Hauser staggered into his house, bleeding heavily from a stab wound in his ribs. He explained that a labourer had brought him a message asking him to meet someone in the Hofgarten. There a man with dark whiskers and a black cloak had asked him, "Are you Caspar Hauser?" When he said yes, the man handed him a silk purse, and then stabbed him in the side. The purse was found in the Hofgarten, and contained an incoherent note signed MLO. It said that Hauser would be able to identify his assailant, who came from a place on the Bavarian border. The name of the place was illegible. Hauser died on 17 December 1833 without having been able to throw any light on the identity of his murderer.

From the moment of his appearance in Nuremberg, controversy had raged around Caspar Hauser. There were many theories as to his origins; but most people believed that he was the illegitimate son of some noble family, and had been kept a prisoner to conceal the dishonour until he became too big to remain locked away. Jacques Bergier, a French writer on the occult, has another theory that is shared by many students of enigmas. It would explain the mysterious appearance of the green children as well as that of Caspar Hauser. Bergier suggests that, for many centuries, the earth has been under study by certain extraterrestrial intelligences. "In my opinion," he says, "after the period of simply auditing and recording what happened on earth, came another period, beginning a few centuries ago, in which the Intelligences began to conduct experiments. These experiments consist of introducing beings capable of arousing the most diverse reactions into our midst, and then studying the way we react – the way we study the behaviour of rats in artificial labyrinths."

It was a bright October morning in 1593. On the plaza in front of the palace in Mexico City there was the usual bustle of people and soldiers. One of these army men stood out. He wore a resplendent uniform unlike the others, and he carried a different kind of gun.

When questioned later, the strange soldier said that his orders that morning were to mount guard at the governor's palace in Manila, where he was stationed. "I know very well this is not the governor's palace – and evidently I am not in Manila," he said . . . "But here I am and this is a palace of some kind so I am doing my duty as nearly as possible." The soldier also told the authorities that the governor had been killed the night before.

The soldier couldn't believe that he was thousands of miles away from Manila, and everyone was baffled by his overnight transportation to Mexico City. The man with this incredible tale was put in jail.

Two months afterwards a ship arrived from the Philippines. It brought news that the governor had been murdered – on the night before the soldier had appeared. The soldier was released and sent back to Manila. Some 400 years later his marvellous trip through space and time remains a mystery.

One day in August 1887 near the small village of Banjos, Spain, a boy and girl walked out of a cave. Some peasants working in a field saw them, and were utterly amazed. The two children had skin as green as grass!

When seen closer, the children were found to have almond-shaped eyes of an Asiatic type. They could not speak Spanish, and they wore clothes of a material never before seen in the Spain of the nineteenth century. No one could understand their language, and no one could analyse the fabric. For five days the boy and girl would not eat any of the various foods brought to them. Finally they began to eat beans. By then the boy was so weakened that he died, but the girl survived. The green colour of her skin gradually faded.

After learning some Spanish, the girl described the country she came from and how she had left it. Her story only made the mystery deeper. She said her native land had no sun at all, and was separated from a sunny land by a river. One day a sudden whirlwind had lifted her and the boy and deposited them in the cave.

The green girl of Banjos lived for only five years more. The mystery of how she and the boy had appeared in Spain was never solved.

Chapter Twenty-Three

Miracles of St Medard

In May 1727 François de Pâris, a young deacon of Paris, died of malnutrition and exhaustion. He was famous for his ascetic practices and for his charities to the poor, and his coffin was followed by hundreds of mourners. After it had been placed behind the altar of the church of St Medard, a line of mourners filed past. One small boy, accompanied by his father, limped awkwardly on a crippled leg. As he placed a bunch of flowers on the coffin, he suddenly fell to the ground, gasping and kicking. He was apparently suffering from a fit. A few minutes later, the fit passed off. The boy sat up, and was helped to his feet. A look of astonishment came over his face. Suddenly he began to dance and shout for joy. The crippled leg – twisted since birth – was straight. As the spectators stared in amazement, an old woman shouted: "I can use it!" She was waving her cured arm, which had been paralysed for twenty-five years. Many fell on their knees around the coffin of the saintly deacon and prayed.

The miracles continued, and became more astounding. All kinds of sick people touched the coffin, went into convulsions, and were cured. After the body of the saintly priest had been buried behind the high altar, the miracles took place in the cemetery outside. They were so remarkable that it is tempting to dismiss contemporary accounts of them as pure exaggerations. Yet documentary evidence – some of it written by physicians – seems to show otherwise. A Mademoiselle Coirin had a cancer that had eaten away most of her breast, and the odour was so appalling that no one could go near her. After kneeling at the "saint's" tomb, not only was she cured, but the breast showed no sign of ever having had a cancer. This sounds absurd, but doctors examined it and testified that it was so.

Cripples walked; the blind were made to see; tumours vanished. Even odder manifestations began to occur. A young girl named Gabrielle Moler went into convulsions, after which she begged the spectators to beat her with sticks. She felt no pain and showed no bruises. She had seemingly acquired some of the curious powers possessed by Hindu fakirs. Strong men could pound her with hammers, and she remained unhurt. She would thrust her face into a blazing fire, and withdraw it unburned; she would leave her feet in the fire until the shoes and socks were burned away, and withdraw her feet unscathed. Another *convulsionaire*, the name given to those who experienced convulsions at the tomb, cured horrible sores and ulcers by sucking them. One man, who had been crippled, experienced the urge to spin on one leg at tremendous speed while reading from a holy book. He did this twice a day. Another *convulsionaire* could bounce six feet into the air, like a rubber ball, even when weighed down with heavy chains. Dozens of other visitors to the tomb rolled in convulsions or allowed spectators to beat them, without visible ill-effects.

A magistrate went to the churchyard convinced that the whole affair was a fraud. What he saw made him change his mind. He wrote books about it, and suffered imprisonment for his convictions.

The authorities were worried and embarrassed by the wild scenes at St Medard. François de Pâris, the young deacon who had started it all, had belonged to a religious sect known as the Jansenists. They denied free will and believed that people could only be saved by Divine Grace. The Jesuits, the most powerful religious order in Paris, detested the Jansenists. Through their influence, the churchyard of St Medard was closed down in 1732, five years after the miracles began. *Convulsionaires* were persecuted, and the miracles ceased. Jansenism was made illegal, and finally died out.

Does a place of worship have more intense thought fields than ordinary buildings? Can this explain the incredible case of the doll with human hair that keeps on growing?

The story comes from northern Japan and started in 1938. In that year Eikichi Suzuki took a ceramic doll to the temple in the village of Monji-Saiwai Cho for safe keeping. It had been a treasured possession of his beloved sister Kiku, who had died nineteen years before at the age of three. Suzuki kept it carefully in a box with the ashes of his dead sister.

Suzuki went off to World War II and didn't return for the doll until 1947. When he opened the box in the presence of the priest, they discovered that the doll's hair had grown down to its shoulders. A skin specialist from the Hokkaido University medical faculty said it was human hair.

The doll was placed on the altar, and its hair continued to grow. It is still growing, and is now almost waist length. The temple has become a place of pilgrimage for worshippers who believe the doll is a spiritual link with Buddha.

The priest of Monji-Saiwai Cho thinks that the little girl's soul somehow continues to live through the doll she loved so much.

Chapter Twenty-Four

Lough Nahooin Monster

L ough Nahooin is a small brown-coloured lake in Connemara on the west coast of Ireland. At 7 o'clock on the evening of 22 February 1968 Stephen Coyne, a local farmer, was walking along the shores of the lough. He was accompanied by his eight-year-old son and his dog. Stopping beside a heap of peat, Coyne saw a black object in the water, and assumed that his dog had gone for a swim. When he whistled, however, the dog came running from the opposite direction and, on seeing the black object began to bark furiously. The farmer looked more closely and saw that the object was some kind of animal with a long neck and shiny black skin. When it plunged its head under the surface, two humps appeared. The farmer also caught a glimpse of a flat tail. By this time the barking of the dog had attracted the attention of the "monster"; it began to swim towards the shore, its mouth open. Alarmed for the safety of his dog, the farmer hurried towards the water. At this the creature turned and made off. The eight-year-old boy ran back to the nearby farm, and brought his mother and the four other Coyne children. The family stood at the edge of the lough watching the monster until it became too dark to see. Describing it later to an investigator, F. W. Holiday, the Coynes said the monster was about twelve feet long. It had no eyes, but there were two horns like those of a snail on top of its head.

H oliday was the author of a book on the famous Loch Ness monster, which he believed to be some kind of giant slug. From the descriptions of the Coyne family, he had no doubt that this Lough Nahooin monster was another member of the same species. Since Lough Nahooin is a mere hundred yards long – compared with the twenty-four miles of Loch Ness – there seemed a reasonable chance of catching the Irish lake monster. Accordingly, Holiday's team brought nets, support-buoys, and a hundred yards of heavy chain to Lough Nahooin. They stretched the nets across the middle of the lake, and then rowed around the lake firing a heavy rifle into the water to force the monster to rush into the nets. Nothing happened – except that Holiday developed a severe toothache. After several disappointing days, they abandoned the hunt. Nevertheless, Holiday remained convinced that the monster had been in the lake all the time – and is there still.

Holiday himself has acknowledged the obvious argument against his idea. Lough Nahooin is full of trout, and if a creature even the size of a crocodile lived there, the fish would all be eaten in a matter of weeks. Perhaps, then, the Coyne family mistook an otter or a large eel for the monster. Even if that were so in this case, there have been numerous sightings of some unknown species in many of the peaty lakes in the west of Ireland. Holiday gathered further evidence from Georgina Carberry, the librarian of Clifden in Connemara. In 1954 Miss Carberry and three friends drove to nearby Lough Fadda, a mile-and-a-half-long lake, to fish for trout. They settled down on a tongue of land to have a picnic. Then they saw the monster, which at first they took to be a man swimming. The creature moved towards them in a leisurely manner, and they could see two large humps and a forked tail. They also saw a huge sharklike mouth, although none of them noticed teeth. When they became alarmed and moved away from the edge of the lake, the creature turned and swam away. Georgina Carberry found the experience so unpleasant that she kept looking back as they drove away to see if the monster was following them. She suffered from nightmares for weeks afterwards, and one of her companions subsequently had a mental breakdown. Miss Carberry described the creature's movements as "wormy". Other witnesses who have reported seeing monsters in nearby lakes generally agree on an undulating wormlike movement.

Strange Tales and Weird Mysteries

Our original objection remains to all such monster sightings: how could creatures of the size described exist in these tiny lakes? Many writers on the Loch Ness monster have made the same point. It is true that Loch Ness is twenty-four miles long, but it is only a mile wide. There would have to be more than one monster for the species to survive, and a colony of monsters would soon eat all the fish and die of starvation.

A few months after his visit to Lough Nahooin, Holiday was browsing through a book on Babylonian history by Sir Wallis Budge. He came across a Babylonian creation myth that described how the god Anu had created marshes. According to the ancient text, "the marshes created the Worm. And the Worm said: '. . . Let me drink amongst the teeth, and set me on the gums, that I may devour the blood of the teeth . . .'" Holiday recalled the strange and persistent toothache that had begun as soon as he arrived at Lough Nahooin, and which vanished as soon as he left the area. He experienced a sudden absurd suspicion: could it be that the monster was not a creature of flesh and blood, *but some kind of a ghost*?

Chapter Twenty-Five

The Statue of Ho-tei

The year was 1928. The city, Kobe, Japan. A middle-aged English couple, the C. J. Lamberts, stood in front of a junk shop window. "That's what I'd like," said Marie Lambert, pointing to a tiny statuette of a half-naked fat man seated on a cushion. She recognized the laughing man as Ho-tei, the Japanese god of Good Luck. "Let's find out what he costs," said her husband, as they walked into the shop. They were pleasantly surprised to find that the statuette was cheap, even though it was made of ivory. It seemed almost too good to be true. Back on their cruise ship, the Lamberts examined their purchase closely. The statuette had the creamy colour of old ivory, and was beautifully carved. As far as they could see, its only imperfection was a small hole underneath. The carver had apparently used the base of an elephant's tusk for the statue, and there was a tiny hole where the nerve of the animal's tooth had ended. This had been plugged neatly with an ivory peg. Altogether, the statuette seemed to be one of those rare bargains that tourists dream about.

Marie Lambert stowed the statuette in her luggage, and the ship sailed to Manila. On the second day out, Mrs Lambert began to suffer from a toothache. The ship's doctor prescribed painkillers, but they did little good. The next twelve days were miserable for both the Lamberts. In Manila, before Mrs Lambert could visit a dentist, she and her husband contracted an unpleasant fever whose chief symptom was pain in all the joints. When Marie Lambert finally got to a dentist, his drill slipped and drove through to the nerve of her tooth, increasing her pain instead of curing it.

177

On the next lap of the voyage, which took the ship to Australia, the god of luck figurine was somehow transferred to Mr Lambert's luggage. The following day, he was prostrated with an agonizing toothache. In Cairns, Australia, he went to a dentist, who told him there was nothing wrong with his teeth. In fact, the ache had stopped while he was at the dentist's. But it started again as soon as he got back to his cabin. Two days later, he consulted another dentist, and the same thing happened. In Brisbane, he ordered a dentist to start pulling out his teeth, and to keep on pulling until the pain stopped. When the first tooth came out, the pain went away. It started again as soon as Lambert returned to the ship.

In Sydney the Lamberts left their luggage in bond. The toothache ceased. On the voyage to New Zealand, the luggage was in their cabin only once, when they repacked; Lambert's toothache started again. Then the luggage went to the hold, and the pain stopped. In New Zealand, while on shore, he had no toothache. There was only one short bout of toothache on the continuing trip to Chile – when the Lamberts repacked their luggage in the cabin. In the United States, the couple visited Lambert's mother. She was so delighted with Ho-tei that they made her a present of the little god. When her excellent teeth started aching a few hours later, she handed back the gift saying that she felt it was "bad medicine". The Lamberts still did not connect Ho-tei with their toothaches.

Their first suspicion occurred on the way across the Atlantic to Britain. A fellow passenger who was interested in ivory borrowed Ho-tei overnight to show her husband. In the morning, she told the Lamberts that she and her husband had both had toothaches. The Lamberts thought about their own toothaches, and realized that they had always occurred when Ho-tei was in their cabin. Marie Lambert wanted to throw the statuette overboard. Her husband was afraid that the god might retaliate by rotting every tooth in their heads.

So they took Ho-tei back to London with them. Lambert took the figure to an oriental art shop and showed it to the Japanese manager, who immediately offered to buy it. Lambert explained that he could not take money for the statuette, and he described the troubles it seemed to have caused. The manager sent for an old man in Japanese national costume, and the two men examined the figure carefully. From what they told him, Lambert gathered that Ho-tei was a temple god. In the East, the statues of such gods are sometimes given "souls" – small medallions hidden inside them. This probably explained the ivory plug in the base of the figure. The old Japanese man placed Ho-tei in a shrine at the end of the shop and lit joss sticks in front of it. Then, with an expression of awe, he bowed Lambert out of the shop.

It is worth recalling that F. W. Holiday complained of a severe toothache during his expedition to Lough Nahooin in search of monsters, and that he subsequently discovered a Babylonian text describing a supernatural worm whose activities include "devouring the blood of the teeth". Is it conceivable that certain negative psychic forces manifest themselves in the form of toothache?

The home of Eugene Binkowski of Rotterdam, New York, had a hum that never stopped. The family wasn't sure when it had started, but became aware of it after a series of illnesses had afflicted each of them. Not only did they have frequent headaches, earaches, and toothaches, but they also suffered from stiffness of the joints. Finally they realized that the source of the problems was a constant faint humming sound throughout the house. They reported the trouble to the police, who could not come up with any explanation.

It was natural that General Electric in nearby Schenectady should become interested in the sound mystery, so the next investigators were technicians from that firm. Using the latest equipment that they had at their command, they tested the house thoroughly. At the end of it, they claimed they could hear no sound of a peculiar nature in the house.

In desperation Binkowski wrote to the then President John Kennedy. A few days later some Air Force sound experts turned up with equipment designed to detect high frequency sounds. They could not trace the hum. The only bit of information they offered was that tests showed the whole family had especially acute hearing. It was possible, they said, for the Binkowskis to be hearing a sound at some unusual pitch. Despite the verdicts of the General Electric and Air Force experts, hundreds of visitors to the Binkowski home reported they could hear the hum. Some of them also felt the house to be mysteriously stuffy.

The Binkowskis endured the hum for about nine months without relief. They finally had to move out of the house and into a garage to escape it.

Chapter Twenty-Six

The Witch
from Next Door

T. C. Lethbridge was trained as an archaeologist and historian, and spent most of his adult life as the Keeper of Anglo-Saxon Antiquities at the University Museum in Cambridge. But even in this respectable setting, he was always upsetting his colleagues. They were particularly shocked at the rumour that he used a dowsing-rod or a pendulum to try to locate objects buried underground. Finally, he left Cambridge in disgust at the hostile reception of one of his books on archaeology. Together with his wife Mina, he moved into Hole House, an old Tudor mansion on the south coast of Devon. He meant to spend his retirement reading and digging for bits of broken pottery. In fact, the most amazing period of his eventful life was about to begin.

The person who was most responsible for this change of direction was an old "witch" who lived next door. This white-haired little old lady assured Lethbridge that she could put mild spells on people who annoyed her, and that she was able to leave her body at night and wander around the district – an ability known as "astral projection". Lethbridge was naturally sceptical – until something convinced him.

The witch explained to him one day how she managed to put off unwanted visitors. What she did was to draw a five-pointed star – a pentagram – in her head, and then visualize it across the path of the unwanted visitor – for example, on the front gate.

Shortly afterwards, Tom was lying in bed, idly drawing pentagrams in his head, and imagining them around their beds. In the middle of the night, Mina woke up with a creepy feeling that there was somebody else in the room. At the foot of the bed, she could see a faint glow of light, which slowly faded as she watched it. The next day, the witch came to see them. When she told them that she had "visited" their bedroom on the previous night, and found the beds surrounded by triangles of fire, Tom's scepticism began to evaporate. Mina politely requested the old witch to stay out of their bedroom at night.

Three years later, the old lady died in peculiar circumstances. She was quarrelling with a neighbouring farmer, and told Lethbridge that she intended to put a spell on the man's cattle. By this time, Lethbridge knew enough about the "occult" to take her seriously, and he warned her about the dangers of black magic – how it could rebound on to the witch. But the old lady ignored his advice. One morning, she was found dead in her bed in circumstances that made the police suspect murder. And the cattle of two nearby farms suddenly got foot and mouth disease. However, the farmer she wanted to "ill wish" remained unaffected. Lethbridge was convinced that the spell had gone wrong and "bounced back".

But the old lady's death resulted – indirectly – in one of his most important insights. Passing the witch's cottage, he experienced a "nasty feeling", a suffocating sense of depression. With a scientist's curiosity, he walked around the cottage, and noticed an interesting thing. He could step *into* the depression and then out of it again, just as if it was some kind of invisible wall.

People in the Welsh town of Wrexham and the surrounding countryside were startled to see hay flying under its own power one ordinary summer day in the late nineteenth century.

According to an account carried in the newspaper, the event occurred at 2 p.m. on a calm July day.

Suddenly some haymakers on a farm saw about half a ton of hay sailing above them through the sky. They said it was higher than they had even seen a crow fly.

The flying hay moved in a northerly direction, which was somewhat surprising because it was going against the wind. Although the mass separated slowly as it covered more distance, it travelled at least five miles without falling apart entirely. It had risen from a field about five miles from Wrexham and had flown over that town at some point in its flight. As the article said, "it caused much consternation while passing over the town."

At the end of this flight of hay, wisps lay here and there along its route. One large clump fell in the middle of a field some distance from the point at which the half-ton mass had first taken to the sky.